Praise for *The* [barcode: T0089596]

"In untangling the threads behind his daughter's suicide, Brooks has transformed his grief into something useful: a warning and a testimony, and, one hopes, a start toward more sensitive treatment of adopted children."

—*The Boston Globe*

"In his first book, Brooks shares his search for answers about his adopted daughter and the unknown childhood trauma that drove her to suicide at age seventeen. The author and his wife, Erika, knew when they adopted Casey that she had been premature, her twin had died at birth, and that she had spent two months in an incubator. . . . The author's description of their anguish is heart-wrenching, and his desperate search for answers and guilt for not doing the right thing without knowing what it was reveals the utter helplessness of suicide survivors. . . .

Brooks explains Casey's disorder and available help in terms that will help anyone struggling with a difficult child. Teachers, analysts, and parents alike can find relief and hope in this book."

—*Kirkus Reviews*

"Rarely have the subjects of suicide, adoption, adolescence, and parenting been explored so openly and honestly."

—John Bateson, former executive director,
Contra Costa Crisis Center, and author of
*The Final Leap: Suicide on the Golden Gate Bridge*

"A must-read for anyone who has adopted or plans to adopt."

—Nancy Newton Verrier, author of
*The Primal Wound* and *Coming Home to Self*

"This is the story of a family like many. Years ago they came together with love and hopefulness. They were determined and uncertain, courageous and afraid and ultimately, innocent and guilty. Do not think that because this is a book about an adoptive family that you will not recognize yourself. Do not think that because it is about a child's suicide that you can have the luxury of turning away. . . . Read this book."

—Anne Brodzinsky, Ph.D., author of *The Mulberry Bird*

"I wish all agencies doing international adoptions made this book required reading. As tragic as this story is, I think it is all too common."

—Eileen McQuade, American Adoption Congress

"When I discovered that my fifteen-year-old son was suicidal, and that my enormous love was never going to be 'enough,' I was fortunate enough to work with an adoption therapist, who is herself adopted. John's compelling and tragic story holds this lesson for all of us, it is crucial to find a therapist who understands in-depth the issues of adoption. They do exist, not in great numbers, and it can be the difference between life and death. I have such enormous respect for John and his willingness to share his story—it will save other lives."

—Jane Ballback, publisher and executive editor,
*Adoption Voices Magazine*

"With its anguished suspense-like telling and lessons learnable, *The Girl Behind the Door* is a book to get wrapped up in."

—*Marco Island Eagle*

# The Girl
# Behind the Door

*A Father's Quest to Understand*
*His Daughter's Suicide*

## John Brooks

SCRIBNER

New York   London   Toronto   Sydney   New Delhi

SCRIBNER
An Imprint of Simon & Schuster, Inc.
1230 Avenue of the Americas
New York, NY 10020

For information about special discounts for bulk purchases,
please contact Simon & Schuster Special Sales at 1-866-506-1949
or business@simonandschuster.com.

The Simon & Schuster Speakers Bureau can bring authors to your live event.
For more information or to book an event, contact the Simon & Schuster Speakers Bureau
at 1-866-248-3049 or visit our website at www.simonspeakers.com.

Manufactured in the United States of America

1   3   5   7   9   10   8   6   4   2

Library of Congress Control Number: 2015032890

ISBN 978-1-5011-2834-9
ISBN 978-1-5011-2836-3 (pbk)
ISBN 978-1-5011-2838-7 (ebook)

*To my daughter, Casey, who whispered in my ear,*
*"Dad, you need to write this book."*
*So I did.*

*All I know she sang a little while*
*and then flew on . . .*

—The Grateful Dead from *Birdsong*,
a tribute to the late Janis Joplin

# ONE

Tuesday, January 29, was the start of another school week after a three-day weekend. It was a dark, blustery, wet morning—typical for a Bay Area winter. My alarm clock went off at six o'clock, but I was too tired to move, enjoying the warmth of a thick down comforter after a fitful night's sleep. I opened one eye and squinted, but all I could see without my glasses was a blurry lump lying next to me. Erika was sound asleep, her dark, shoulder-length hair tousled, her face pressed into her hypo-allergenic pillow. She wheezed peacefully through her stuffy nose.

I closed my eyes and rolled over. Just another thirty minutes and then I'd get up. Within minutes, I fell into a mini-dream. I was in an old mansion with a maze of hallways, trying to get out so that I could go home. The more hallways I tried, looking for the front door, the further I sank into confusion. I yelled for help but no sound came out of my mouth.

My eyes blinked open.

Squinting at the red display on the alarm clock in the half-light, I saw that it was 6:35; I was late. I sat up and put my glasses on, surveying the room. Igor, our dog, was a heap of legs in front of our bed. His skinny, whippet racer's hindquarters rested on his sleeping pad while his head and front paws spilled over onto the floor. He opened one of his dark, bulging eyes, following my movements as I got my bearings. With his long, pointy nose, delicate flappy ears, and those big eyes, he looked like a friendly deer.

He'd slept with us that night so that our daughter, Casey, could be left alone in her room. We'd had a nasty fight over the last few days that had left everyone exhausted. She'd been grounded all weekend over her complete disrespect for us and for her continuing use of foul language. Another battle of wills between an angry teenager and her parents.

I left the bedroom, heading down the hallway that opened into our great room to my left: a living room, dining room, and kitchen all flowing into one large, airy space. Straight ahead of me, the hallway split into a T, my office to the left and Casey's room and her bathroom to the right. An oversize Keith Haring poster, with its graffiti-inspired cartoonish shapes, hung at the junction of the T.

Instead of turning left toward the kitchen, I headed for Casey's room and stopped at her door, or what was left of it. She'd suffered from violent tantrums and meltdowns since she was an infant, thrashing, screaming, wailing, and pummeling that door until cracks opened in the seams. I'd vowed not to replace it again until she left to start college in September, just nine months away.

I put my ear to the door and heard music, faint and tinny, as if it were coming from a toy speaker. I knocked lightly. Should I let her be late for school and suffer the consequences? No. I didn't want to add to the tension in the house by letting her be late out of spite. First period at Redwood High School started at eight o'clock. If she got up now I could drop her off on my way to work.

"Casey? You up?"

Nothing.

I cracked the door open and peeked in. The darkened room seemed neater than usual. I could actually see the blue-gray carpet, stained from spilled food, coffee, and Igor's vomit. Her clothes were piled neatly on her bamboo papasan chair in the corner and her bed was made.

On the bedside table, her clock radio had been set to the local hip-hop station. The irritating beat of gangster rap drifted from its small plastic speaker; the red display flashed 5:00. That was odd. What could she have been doing up at five in the morning?

Feeling uneasy, I turned off the radio and left for the living room. When I went to bed the night before, she'd been encamped on the burgundy leather sofa watching *America's Next Top Model* on Bravo, at the same time drumming away furiously on her laptop, probably chatting with a friend online. But in the gray of the winter morning, the sofa was empty. The cable remote lay on the floor, an open can of Diet Dr Pepper on the coffee table. No coaster under it, of course.

I headed for my office. Sometimes she'd fall asleep on the futon bed. But she wasn't there either.

My pulse quickened as I hurried back through the living room to the front door. Outside, the darkened street, still wet from rain, lit by streetlamps, was where I'd parked the Saab the day before.

It was gone.

I felt a surge of anger. How was I going to get to work? Erika needed our other car, the family SUV, to get to her job. But irritation turned to fear as the reality of Casey's disappearance sank in. She could storm out of the house and stalk around the neighborhood smoking a cigarette and griping to her friends on her cell phone. But she'd never done anything like this; never gotten up this early, never taken my car.

I rushed back to her room. In the half-light I caught sight of a spiral pad of thick white parchment paper for sketching watercolors. It was open to a short note that Casey had written in green ink with her minuscule, precise lettering sloping slightly downward from left to right, a trademark of left-handed writers.

*The car is parked at the Golden Gate Bridge. I'm sorry.*

My body froze as I stared at the words *Golden Gate Bridge*. The blood drained from my face, the air sucked from my lungs.

I hurried back to our bedroom. Erika was buried under the comforter and a pile of pillows. I touched her arm. "Honey, you need to get up." I struggled for calm. "There's something wrong with Casey."

"What? What?" Erika lifted her head, alarmed and confused. She wore a T-shirt, pajama pants, and ankle socks. Her feet were always cold.

"Her room's empty. The car's gone."

She kicked off the covers and groped the bedside table for her glasses. Igor was jolted off his sleeping pad, shivering nervously, fixing an anxious look on us.

"Maybe she went to a friend's house," she said, still trying to absorb my words.

"Honey, she left this." My hand trembled as I held out the note.

"Oh my God. No!" Her face was frozen in terror. I picked up the bedside phone. It was 6:40, just ten minutes since I'd gotten up.

"Nine-one-one. What's your emergency?"

The words tumbled out of my mouth.

"My name is John Brooks. I live at 15 Claire Way in Tiburon.

My daughter Casey's disappeared. She left a note saying that she left the car at the Golden Gate Bridge parking lot."

"Okay. Sir, please try to calm down. What kind of car is it?"

"A red 1999 Saab 9-3."

"And you said the Golden Gate Bridge parking lot?"

"Yes. I'm assuming the southbound lot on the Marin side."

"Can you describe her to me? Do you know what she was wearing?"

"She's seventeen, about five-five, five-six, thin, with brown hair cut shoulder length. I don't know what she was wearing."

"Sir, when did you last see her?"

I returned to that last image of her, sulking on the sofa the night before, ignoring me.

*Jesus, was this about that fight we had last weekend?*

"In the house at around ten thirty last night."

"All right, sir. Please stay where you are. An officer will be there in a few minutes. We're contacting the Golden Gate Bridge Patrol and the CHP to check on the location of the car."

I hung up, stunned and light-headed. Erika and I were disoriented, looking at each other, racked with fear, unable to concentrate. I sat on the edge of the bed, staring at a photograph on my dresser. It was Casey's formal eighth-grade prom portrait. She wore a white party dress with red trim that showed off her bare neck and shoulders. Her hair—then blond—was tied back, her braces were off, and her hazel eyes were highlighted with mascara and eyeliner. She had a self-conscious smile but to me she was a knockout.

*Think, God damn it!*

I hurried back to Casey's room to look for her phone. Her friends should have known where she was. But it was only 6:45, too early. They'd be pissed at me for waking them up and freaking them out at this hour if this turned out to be nothing. I scanned her room.

Her phone was gone, along with her wallet and pocketbook; not the expensive Marc Jacobs handbag we'd bought together in Greenwich Village the year before for her seventeenth birthday, but the cheaper, everyday knock-around one. I rushed back to the kitchen where Erika, now dressed in jeans and a sweatshirt, paced aimlessly.

"Honey, I'm dialing Casey's cell." Erika looked at me, lost.

The standard greeting voice answered, *"Please leave your message for . . ."* and then Casey's voice, *"Quasey."* That was the nickname bestowed on her by her friends. It was short for Quasimodo, the Hunchback of Notre Dame, in reference to Casey's slouchy posture, but all the kids slouched.

"Casey, it's Dad. Do you have your phone? Where are you? We have your note. Please call me. Everyone's looking for you." I paused for a moment. "Honey, we love you." Another pause. Lacking more words, I pressed END.

At 6:50 the doorbell rang. I opened it to an officer from the Tiburon Police Department. His white-and-blue cruiser was parked on the street behind him. He was young, maybe late twenties, average height, with a strong build and blond hair shaved close, military style. Igor sidled up and sniffed his uniform.

"Mr. Brooks? I'm Officer Gilbreath." He looked familiar.

In the living room, Erika and I gave him a quick rundown of the last twenty minutes. The young officer's expression grew somber. He asked to see Casey's room and I led him in, hoping he wouldn't notice the battered door. He looked around for a minute but found nothing helpful. His radio crackled with a garbled voice, but he ignored it.

"Officer, what's going on with the car down by the bridge?" I asked, my mind still racing. "We have to go down there."

"The CHP's been dispatched to look for it. They'll contact us when they find something. But sir, you really need to stay put."

"I'm sorry, Officer. We can't stay here. We have to go to the bridge."

He thought for a moment. "Okay. Is there a neighbor or friend nearby I can contact?"

I gestured toward the house next door. "Our neighbors Jerry and Laura. They should be home."

I needed to use the bathroom before we left. As I splashed water on my face, I studied the person in the mirror staring back at me. He looked like he'd busted out of a mental institution— hair like some kind of fright wig, eyes bloodshot, eyelids puffy, every flaw magnified.

Returning to the living room, I gave Gilbreath my cell phone number as Erika and I hustled out the door. We stumbled into our SUV for the eight-mile trip down the 101 freeway to the Golden Gate Bridge.

It was 7:10, rush hour. As we drove, I glanced at other drivers around us in their BMWs, Mercedeses, and Jaguars. Just another Tuesday-morning commute into San Francisco. Their impassive faces suggested nothing was wrong.

For a moment, I felt a wild sense of relief. Casey was proba- bly at a friend's house. She'd show up later, apologizing for taking the car without permission. Or maybe she did go to the bridge in a dramatic impulse but changed her mind and was already on her way home.

We emerged from the Waldo Tunnel—a hole bored through the Marin Headlands—to the Golden Gate Bridge in front of us, shrouded in fog, with the bay and the city in the background like a Department of Tourism poster. Normally, this would have been the highlight of my commute to work in San Francisco's financial district, but that morning the fog-shrouded bridge looked cold and menacing.

We pulled into the parking lot at the north end of the bridge at 7:20 and there it was—my red Saab. A black California Highway Patrol cruiser was parked behind it, its engine idling. We stared in disbelief at the Saab and the CHP cruiser as I killed the ignition. She *had* come to the bridge.

We both got out. A CHP officer got out of the cruiser to meet us. "Mr. and Mrs. Brooks? I'm Officer Shipman."

My mind was in overdrive. "Officer, has anyone seen Casey?"

"I got here about twenty minutes ago," Shipman said. "The engine was warm to the touch, so it probably hasn't been here that long."

Erika's voice was high, strained. "What are you doing to find her?"

Shipman remained calm and businesslike. "Mrs. Brooks, we've sent out an APB for a juvenile risk. The U.S. Park Police, Coast Guard, Bridge Patrol, and CHP have all been dispatched to look for your daughter."

The doors to the Saab were locked, so I used my key fob to open them. Casey's new iPhone—a Christmas present from my mother—and a lighter were on the front passenger seat. A pack of Camel Lights was stowed in the center console cubbyhole. I hated the fact that she smoked.

Her pocketbook was on the floor in front of the passenger seat. I emptied its contents onto the seat—her wallet, makeup, lipstick, Kleenex, Orbit gum, wads of blank notebook paper, matches, loose change—but still no clues. Likewise, nothing in the trunk.

I grabbed her phone and clicked Contacts. I knew a few of Casey's friends, but never said much more than a polite "hello" or "goodbye" as they hurried off through the living room to her bedroom. We were under strict orders to never talk to her friends.

I saw her friend Max's name under Recent Calls. I remembered Max. He was a tall, skinny kid with wild, curly hair. They'd been friends since kindergarten. My thumb punched furiously at his name on the glass screen and finally connected, but the call went to voice mail.

Then I saw her friend Julian's name. He was a nice kid, slightly built, cute. They were best friends and hung around a lot. Casey would often head over to his house when she needed to dowse the fire from the pain of one of her meltdowns.

"Yo, Quasey. 'Sup homes?" He sounded wide-awake and ready for school.

"Julian, it's Casey's dad, John. Listen, Casey disappeared this morning. She took the car to the Golden Gate Bridge. I'm here now. Do you know where she might be?"

The phone was silent for a moment. When he spoke, the playfulness in his voice had vanished. "Wow. No, I'm sorry. I have no idea. What's going on?"

"Thanks, Julian. I gotta go."

*Shit! Shit! Shit!*

My BlackBerry rang. "Mr. Brooks, it's Officer Gilbreath. We need you to come back to the house . . . now."

Without even asking why he wanted us to come home, I replied, "Okay, we'll be there in about ten minutes." I couldn't detect anything in his voice that indicated whether he had good or bad news. I tried to be upbeat. He didn't say anything. Maybe it wasn't what I feared.

We drove home in tense silence. Erika clung tightly to her

pocketbook in her lap, her knuckles white. As we pulled up to the house, we saw a second white-and-blue Tiburon Police cruiser parked on the street.

We walked through the door to find more people inside. In addition to Officer Gilbreath, there was a more senior officer, Sergeant Hayes. They stood stiffly in the living room, their eyes locked on us. Our neighbors Jerry and Laura stood next to them in a semicircle. They stared at us, pained looks on their faces. Something ominous.

Officer Gilbreath motioned with his hand for us to sit down. Erika took a seat on the sofa next to Laura while I sat next to Jerry. I felt light-headed, disconnected from the people around me, as if I were watching a movie.

The pale yellow of the living room walls captured what little daylight filtered through the clouds. The fireplace in the corner was framed by a mantelpiece that Erika had painted in a bird's-eye maple pattern. Behind the two police officers was the media cabinet filled with books, family photographs, and a wide-screen TV.

Gilbreath had a slight tremor in his hands as he looked down and read from his notepad. He'd spoken with the Golden Gate Bridge Patrol. Homeland Security surveillance videos recorded a dark-colored Saab pulling into the Dillingham parking lot at 6:15. A female exited the car dressed in jogging attire. She took the pedestrian walkway that led under the Golden Gate Bridge to the bay side, which was the more popular destination for joggers, walkers, and tourists to soak in the dramatic view of San Francisco Bay and the city.

I stared unblinking at Gilbreath, with no awareness of anyone else in the room, as he stuck to his notes. I labored to breathe as my heart rate accelerated. My car keys slipped from my hand.

"The female was seen smoking a cigarette while walking. She put it out near the Vista Point parking lot. Then she jogged onto the bridge and stopped in the middle." Gilbreath stopped to clear his throat, his eyes darting up to meet mine before snapping back to his notepad. "She climbed over the four-foot railing to the narrow maintenance platform, stood on the platform for ten to fifteen seconds, and stepped off."

It was 6:40 when Casey jumped, just about the time I called 911. She left the keys to the Saab behind on the railing.

# TWO

Katarina was thirty-six, unmarried and pregnant. She already had two children. They lived in her parents' house 160 miles north of Warsaw in the Masurian Lake District, a resort area known as the "summer capital of Poland."

On the night of May 3, 1990, Katarina went into labor six weeks early. Her father bundled her into the family car for the short trip to the nearest public hospital in Giżycko, the Samodzielny Publiczny Zakład Opieki Zdrowotnej. Her mother stayed behind with the children. Soon after they arrived in the emergency room, Katarina gave birth to a girl, small and weak, weighing only three pounds, struggling to breathe through lungs that hadn't yet fully developed. The triage nurse rushed the baby to an incubator.

Within seconds, the doctor realized that there was another baby, a twin. She was dead.

The baby in the incubator was named Joanna. She remained in the hospital for two months, protected from human touch until she could breathe on her own. Katarina's parents had persuaded her to give the baby up for adoption. She signed away parental rights to her surviving daughter.

When Joanna was well enough to breathe on her own, she was sent to the Dom Dziecka, the State Home for Children, in the nearby town of Mrągowo. This would be her home for the next year.

# THREE

In July 1991, I had my six-foot-two-inch frame folded into the backseat of a dusty, red Nissan as it headed toward that same State Home for Children. Poland was in the grip of a heat wave, and the Nissan had no air-conditioning, let alone seat belts or legroom. Erika sat next to me, glistening with sweat from the suffocating heat.

Renata, our Polish adoption attorney, sat in the passenger seat in front of me. She was probably in her forties, but the deeply etched circles under her eyes made her appear older. Still, she was an attractive woman, slender with dirty blond, shoulder-length hair. Her husband, Marian, was at the wheel. He acted as chauffeur, concierge, and legal assistant. With his wiry build and angular features he reminded me of a character actor on a 1980s TV show about lawyers in L.A.

He'd been a judge but gave up his career because Renata's adoption practice was so lucrative. Her fee was $15,000, whereas a judge's salary was about $150 a month. Despite the stress that hung over us, they were both pleasant, persistent, and totally professional, practiced in managing jet-lagged and anxious Western parents-to-be.

———

It's a familiar story. After two years of invasive fertility tests, hormone injections, and sex timed to ovulation cycles, Erika and I had accepted that a biological child was probably a long shot for us.

What about adoption?

One bitter cold January evening, we'd attended a support group at a Unitarian Meeting House near our home in Simsbury, Connecticut, for couples seeking alternatives to infertility. We were eager for good news, but the reality was quite different.

We learned that the waiting list for a traditional adoption through a public agency stretched up to ten years. An independent adoption arranged through an attorney was not only costly but risky because the birth mother could change her mind. A foreign adoption was another alternative, especially for parents willing to consider an older or special needs child, but this was not entirely risk-free. The adoption window could arbitrarily open or close based on political whims and public opinion, and the process could take a year or more while a child we would have begun to love as our own stayed behind in an orphanage. The list of available countries was also limited to a smattering of Far East, Third World, and former Soviet Bloc countries—South Korea, Colombia, Guatemala, Ethiopia, and Romania.

At the conclusion of the presentation, we dragged ourselves toward the door of the Meeting House contemplating an empty life without children—careers, nieces and nephews, hobbies, travel, pets, anything to fill the void of a childless life or, as some called it, a *child-free* life. Then a brochure for a charitable group caught my eye. One word leaped off the page about their list of host countries:

*Poland.* Erika's family was from Poland. Maybe this was our chance.

———

We'd met Renata through a chance connection with our adoption agency, Family & Children's Agency of Greater Norwalk, Connecticut. Another of their clients, a couple in New Haven, had recently adopted a two-year-old Polish girl. Renata was initially hesitant to take us on as clients. Not only did she have a large caseload, but she'd face strong resistance with two American couples because the Polish government had a strong preference for placing its orphaned children with Polish families. Yet in this conservative, Catholic country, orphaned children outnumbered willing adoptive parents. Two Americans were better than no parents at all.

Erika persisted. In late-night phone calls, she told Renata about her parents' experience growing up in occupied Poland. They were teenagers, well educated, with high aspirations when the Nazis—and then the Russians—overran their country. Heavy artillery on the streets became the new normal. They adapted to negotiating with abusive soldiers over seemingly minor things, such as crossing the street to get to the butcher. One brother disappeared, resurfacing later in England. In her textbook Polish, Erika summed up her family history to Renata:

*"My parents watched as their country was torn apart by Germans and Russians. They jumped at the chance to take a boat to America, settled in Detroit, where my father made a good living in the radio business, selling advertising."*

Perhaps Renata was impressed with the story or Erika's efforts to communicate in the difficult Polish language, something

Erika's parents insisted she learn from childhood, rather than default to English. Then Erika played our trump card, something we'd agreed to if it meant that we could adopt a child more quickly and shorten the yearlong wait we'd been warned about.

"We'd be interested in a special needs child."

It was then, after some reflection, that Renata told us about the little infant girl Joanna, then ten months old, in the Dom Dziecka in Mrągowo. She was a preemie, very underdeveloped, and her medical history was limited, but she was available. We couldn't believe our good fortune—a ten-month-old Polish girl was *available*.

———

Just four short months after that encounter, we were bound for Mrągowo. As we sped through the Polish countryside, Erika and Renata carried on a conversation I couldn't understand, but their tone was relaxed—a good sign, I thought. Since we'd arrived in Warsaw three days earlier, my only way of deciphering conversation was to read facial cues and listen for vocal inflections. There was nothing intuitive about this language.

We'd been on the road three hours since they'd picked us up at our hotel in Warsaw. Adding to the misery of the heat, Renata and Marian chain-smoked unfiltered French Gauloises. The smoke hung in a drifting cloud around us in the car, the pungent smell filling my nose, eyes, hair, and clothes.

I felt a crushing headache building between my temples and I needed air, but didn't dare ask them to put out their cigarettes. We were desperate to avoid offending anyone, as if asking to stub out the Gauloises would unravel our carefully orchestrated arrangement. Instead I rolled down my window and let the blast of hot air cleanse my nostrils.

Outside, the asphalt of the road melted under the scorching sun. Cars and trucks left tire tracks in the black goop. A green road sign whizzed by—E77. This was the rough Polish equivalent of an interstate—a two-lane roadway with narrow shoulders on either side, the width of a bicycle lane, for slow-moving farm vehicles.

A silver Porsche with German plates blew past us. I held my breath, watching. It cut back into our lane in front of a Russian Lada up ahead, narrowly averting a head-on collision with a semi overtaking a lumbering green tractor hauling a load of hay the other way. Marian shook his head and gestured with his hands, muttering *"Dupa,"* Polish for "asshole."

We continued through towns with tongue-twisting names such as Nowy Dwór Mazowiecki and Strzegowo, passing ancient Gothic churches, stately municipal buildings, dreary Soviet-era apartment blocks, seedy commercial offices, and grandiose monuments to Polish heroes of so many lost wars. Renata lit another cigarette and blew the smoke out her window. I fished through Erika's pocketbook for two Extra Strength Tylenols.

While waiting for the Tylenol to work its magic on my headache, I unpacked my video camera and pointed it out the window to record our journey for posterity, my mind drifting to the only image we had of Joanna, courtesy of a FedEx package we'd received in March. A single photograph showed a dark-haired young woman with a caring face holding a baby girl who looked like a Michelin man stuffed into two pairs of woolen footie pajamas.

The baby had a pouty look on her face, as if she'd been woken up from a nap just long enough to get her picture taken. Her head was sort of squarish with very little hair, and she had a cute little turned-up nose that was beet red. Maybe she had a sniffle. She didn't look particularly happy, but to us she looked magnificent.

Renata pulled a one-page document out of the worn, stuffed briefcase by her feet and handed it to Erika. She said something in her deep, scratchy voice as Erika took the document. "*Tak.* Okay," she said, nodding. I leaned over Erika's shoulder, trying to read the strange writing.

"It is for taking Joanna out of orphanage," Renata told me.

"Oh. *Dziękuję!* Thank you," I said with a smile, proudly using one of my seven words of Polish.

"*Nie ma za co,*" she answered, smiling at me. Seeing that I didn't understand a word, she repeated in English, "You're welcome."

"Oh, right. *Tak!*" I felt like such an idiot. She turned to Erika and said something in Polish, smiling. Erika laughed. Marian grinned and coughed, his cigarette dangling from his mouth as he drove. Why were they laughing? Erika leaned toward me. "Renata said with a little practice you could speak fluent Polish."

"Very funny."

As we continued farther north we passed forests, lakes, dairy farms, and rolling hills similar to those in Wisconsin. Renata gave us a guided tour of the countryside. "This is the Lake District. Very beautiful. Many people come here on holiday—Germans, Dutch, Danes. For them it is very cheap."

Erika chatted away with Renata while I listened and stared at the scenery, thinking about the laborious steps we'd taken to get to this point. Just six months earlier, we'd walked out of the Unitarian Meeting House with little hope of ever having a child. Now we were just a couple of hours away from meeting the child we would name Casey, which meant "brave." We were about to become parents.

———

From the first conversation Erika had had with Renata about Joanna, we'd worried about her health. We knew that as a preemie, she was underweight and very weak. We'd learned from a pediatric neurologist back home in Connecticut that a ten-month-old infant should have been able to stand, pick up small objects, feed herself, and play simple games. Joanna couldn't even sit up. She appeared to be at the developmental level of a six-month-old, but without an in-person evaluation it was impossible to know if she was simply understimulated or suffered from something more serious such as brain damage or cerebral palsy. Joanna had had perfunctory medical checkups, which were positive, but she'd never been evaluated by a neurologist for the kind of mental or physical problems common to being born premature. We had no way of knowing if there were any other family issues of heart disease, thyroid problems, depression, mental illness, or substance abuse. And the birth father might as well have been a phantom.

In June, before we'd left for Poland, Renata had arranged an evaluation for Joanna with a specialist in the town of Olstyn. We set up a conference call with our neurologist, and with Erika as translator, learned that the Polish doctor had put Joanna through a battery of tests for movement, balance, strength, and coordination. She'd failed them all, yet he was surprisingly upbeat. His theory was that Joanna could have just been weak from lack of stimulation.

Our American neurologist remained unconvinced. But then, he hadn't seen her. On the other hand, as much as I wanted to believe the Polish doctor, I hesitated to put too much faith in him either, someone I'd never met.

—

I checked my watch as we slowed down to get around another tractor moving at fifteen miles per hour up ahead on the E77. It was two thirty. We were supposed to be at the orphanage at three o'clock. Our adoption journey seemed to be set on fast-forward—way too fast for us to process—and now we were minutes away from our daughter. I couldn't imagine what it would be like to hold her, to hear what sounds came out of her mouth, to see what kind of personality she had, how she'd react upon seeing us.

At exactly three o'clock we pulled into Mrągowo, a picturesque town of 23,000 sandwiched between Lake Czos and Lake Juno. Marian headed straight for the Dom Dziecka, where he was to leave us; he would return later to take us to our hotel. As we pulled up to the gate, my heart was in overdrive. I felt a confounding mix of relief that we'd soon see Joanna and a nagging fear that she'd be nothing like what we'd expected. Erika appeared to hide her own nervousness behind a mask that exuded a calm, upbeat, even humorous demeanor. I was always a glass-half-empty kind of guy whereas Erika's glass was always half full.

The orphanage looked like a boarding school—a three-story beige stucco structure with a red tile roof. It must've predated the Soviet era because it didn't fit with the drab, depressing utilitarian concrete blocks that were the trademark of Communist architecture. Big oak and alder trees dotted the grounds. A metal swing set with a slide and a sandbox stood out front. A basketball hoop was mounted to a wall. Some bicycles and three-wheelers lay on the ground. That was reassuring.

Across the street through the thick oak trees Lake Juno glittered in the hot sun. An old man stood fishing along the shore, a young couple paddled a kayak out on the water. It was so tantalizingly close, but did the children ever have a chance to enjoy it?

A group of boys on a second-floor terrace watched our every move. Renata turned around to Erika and said something in Polish. The only words I could make out were *"nie normale."* I assumed it was a reminder that most of the children there were handicapped. She'd told us months before about the special needs kids. My forehead beaded up with perspiration.

*Had Renata been totally truthful with us about Joanna's health, knowing how committed we'd become? There was no way we could turn back now. I could never live with myself if we did. I'd always think about her.*

I studied the boys on the terrace more closely as we pulled up. They stared and pointed at us. Most of them looked to be middle school or high school age. An older boy who appeared to be about sixteen, tall and skinny with an olive complexion, smiled strangely, as if he thought we were there for him. A younger one, maybe ten or eleven, had leg braces and crutches. He threw his twisted body from side to side as he walked, letting go of a crutch to wave at us. Another one sat slumped and shrunken in a wheelchair, expressionless. He looked like he had some kind of neuromuscular disease that had left him paralyzed.

Even though Renata had warned us not to be upset by the children, it was disturbing to see them up close. I felt awkward and guilty, even repelled by them, wondering how often they'd been let down by adoptive parents who'd come and left the orphanage with the younger, more attractive children. I gave them a half-hearted smile and a little wave back from the open car window. They were excited that I had acknowledged their existence, and waved furiously at me, as if trying to say *"Please pick me!"*

Erika didn't seem to be as bothered by the kids on the terrace as I was. She took it in stride, smiled, waved back at them, and grabbed my hand. "This is it." With the image of the handicapped children in my head, I felt another surge of fear over Joanna's health and looked at Erika sitting next to me. She was calm.

*Breathe.*

I said a silent prayer as we stepped out of the car and walked up to the entrance.

# FOUR

A thick, rosy-cheeked woman dressed in a white lab coat greeted us warmly in the foyer. She could have been the director or one of the higher-ups, but Renata told us that she was one of the staff teachers. Her name was Danuta.

As we exchanged nervous smiles, nods, and *dzień dobrys*, Polish for "good day," I looked past Danuta to see what I could of Joanna's home. There were no children in the hallway past the foyer, and I wondered where their living quarters were. Part of me was uneasy with the idea of seeing other rooms in the orphanage or the area where Joanna stayed in her crib. Perhaps it was better that her room remain a product of my imagination rather than risk a letdown by reality.

Danuta seemed jumpy as she hurried us into a reception room, gesturing us toward a sofa, nodding and saying something to Erika I didn't understand while she grabbed a couple of tea-cups and saucers from a cupboard. She seemed just as eager to make a good impression on us as we were on her. What a relief.

I was afraid that they might have been surly and jealous of two Americans snatching one of their children.

The reception room was bright and pleasant, painted a pale shade of pink, almost like a skin tone. There were framed pictures of Polish cartoon characters on the walls—a jaunty cat, a prince on a horse, a queen holding a teacup, a bullfighter on the attack. Some shelves had been crammed with potted plants, books, stuffed animals, and dolls—a big, smiley red-haired clown, a blond doll with pigtails in a pink dress, a set of Russian *matryoshka* dolls arranged neatly in a row. There was a large metal desk in the middle of the room. Danuta sat behind it, Renata next to her in a chair, both of them engrossed in conversation. There was one odd thing in the room—a bathroom sink mounted on the wall in the corner, complete with towels, soap, and shampoo.

Perhaps to conserve energy, the lights were turned off. There was no air-conditioning, not even a fan. The windows were left open to bring in some air, but there was no breeze. With no screens, flies buzzed in and out of the room. A radio in the background played Polish choral music. Everyone in the room perspired from the heat, some of us from nerves.

I was in a daze, light-headed from the language barrier and the two Extra Strength Tylenols. I asked Erika, "What's going on?"

"They're getting her up from her nap, and Danuta asked if we wanted tea."

"What did you say?"

"Yes."

Erika struck up a conversation with Danuta as she made our tea. It sounded like casual small talk. Erika let out a hearty laugh. Danuta laughed along with her and appeared more relaxed. That was a good sign, wasn't it?

"What did you say?" I asked.

"I wanted to know how Joanna was feeling and Danuta said she had a bit of a runny nose. Then I told her I carry all sorts of remedies in my pocketbook wherever I go. So Joanna will be in good hands."

"You mean Casey."

"To them she's still Joanna."

Renata and Danuta huddled over the desk, talking in low voices. Danuta nodded at something Renata said, looking tense.

I leaned in toward Erika. "What are they talking about?"

She strained to hear them. "I'm not sure. Something about getting the documents ready for tomorrow." Thank God for Renata.

Erika pulled a small pink squeaky doll with a white bonnet out of her denim diaper bag. She sat next to me staring silently at it while playing with its arms and legs. Her hair was still big and puffy from the heat, and she fanned herself with the doll. If she was anxious, she didn't show it. The choral music on the radio stopped and I heard an announcer speak, maybe the news.

I put aside my uneasiness over the handicapped kids we'd seen earlier. The ambience of the room was comforting. The warmth and hospitality of the staff felt genuine. This was how I'd hoped it would be.

I set up my video camera on a cabinet and hit the RECORD button. Danuta went to check on Joanna while Erika looked for the bathroom. I was alone with Renata, trying to make small talk, but my mind was elsewhere. Without a cigarette, she was fidgety and looked ill when she spoke to me. "They say all of documents will be ready for us tomorrow morning."

"Oh. *Dobrze.*" I tried out the Polish word for "good," which I'd memorized.

She smiled and nodded. *"Bardzo dobrze."* Seeing the puzzled look on my face, she added, "Very good."

"Oh, right." I felt so stupid trying to make small talk in Polish. We stood awkwardly for a few minutes, Renata looking anxious. The door opened. It was Danuta followed by Erika. I felt more at ease with Erika back, not quite so helpless. Nonetheless my knee bounced uncontrollably. Erika put her arm around me and gave me another reassuring smile and laugh.

"How can you be so calm?" I asked.

"I look calm? I feel like I'm jumping out of my skin. You know I laugh when I'm nervous."

"Right." I clasped her hand. It was cold and damp.

The door opened and we both turned around, expecting someone to come in with Joanna. Instead it was the young woman from the photograph we'd gotten in the FedEx package. I recognized her immediately as the staffer holding Joanna. She was very pretty and every bit as friendly as I imagined her from the photograph.

Erika chatted with her, pointing at herself and then me. The woman smiled, nodding at both of us knowingly. Erika turned to me. "Her name is Karina. She said Joanna will be here in a second. She's getting her diaper changed."

My nerves on edge, I jangled a handful of coins in my pocket, double-checking the video camera to make sure it was recording, imagining the disaster if I'd missed this precious moment. Somewhere a child let out a bloodcurdling scream.

"Maybe that's her," I said to Erika, a nervous joke.

Our tea had been set down on the table but we never touched it.

Another woman in a lab coat appeared. She was older, perhaps in her sixties, with a thick build, pale skin, crooked teeth, and white hair. She carried a quiet infant girl.

It was Joanna.

The white-haired woman held her up to us, smiling proudly as if she were presenting a champion show dog.

I was mesmerized.

Joanna looked just the way she did in the picture, but this time dressed in a pink T-shirt and shorts with dirty white socks on her feet, a size too big. Danuta and Karina perked up and smiled when they saw her, winking and blowing kisses. Everyone seemed especially attached to her.

Erika, Renata, and I crowded around the white-haired woman holding her. She gently passed her silent charge over to Erika, who cradled her in her arms while Joanna remained passive, as if trying to understand the significance of the handoff from her familiar caregiver to some stranger.

Erika cooed *kohana*, "sweetie pie" in Polish, and gave her the pink squeaky doll, which Joanna took and clutched in her chubby little fist. Renata stood back, hands on hips, nodding at Joanna as if to say, *See, isn't she magnificent?* She looked like a proud godmother. I just gazed at Joanna.

She'd changed a bit from the picture we'd received in March. Her head was rounder, with the same turned-up nose, a high prominent forehead, full pink cheeks, and thin red lips. Her eyes were a bluish gray and her sparse blond hair was very fine. If her T-shirt had been blue instead of pink, she could've been mistaken for a beautiful boy. She appeared to have all of her fingers and toes. Nothing looked misshapen or out of place.

She was perfect.

Erika held Joanna in her arms, speaking to her in a Polish baby voice, bouncing her up and down. She seemed to know intuitively what to do as I stood by, feeling a bit shy and self-conscious. This wasn't how I'd imagined it—no beam of light, no blubbering; in fact, nobody shed a tear. I should have felt something but, strangely, I had no emotional sensation at all. It was surreal, like a dream or a movie scene.

Joanna looked to be in as much of a daze as I was. That was understandable, considering that she'd just woken from a nap. She was suffering from a cold and had just been thrust into the arms of two foreigners. Silent and lethargic, she showed no emotion, no smiles or giggles as I'd imagined. She appeared physically fine but her silence worried me. Was that normal?

Joanna stared at me as if I were an alien, her wide eyes following me everywhere as I circled around her like someone inspecting a new car. Wherever I stood, her head turned to follow my every move, still emotionless. Maybe she'd never seen a man before. The orphanage staff seemed composed entirely of women. As we watched each other I let out a nervous laugh. What was she thinking as she kept her eyes locked on me?

Everybody around me talked excitedly, laughing. What were they saying? I felt as if I should have come prepared with questions. What did they know about her mother? Who was the mystery father? How did Joanna spend her day? Was she always this quiet? But my mind froze. I couldn't risk upsetting the mood when things seemed to be going so well. Maybe I was being overly paranoid.

The staffers called her Asia or Joasia—Polish pet names for Joanna. For the first time, Joanna's face lit up with a faint smile when Karina cooed out "Asia" to her as if she were a puppy. Renata patted me on the arm and motioned me closer to Joanna. This whole time, I hadn't even touched her.

"Here, honey, you hold her." Erika handed her to me. "C'mon, she won't break."

I'd had almost no experience holding babies, except for my

nephew, whom I'd held gingerly for a moment before handing him back to his mother, relieved that I hadn't dropped him or made him cry. Grabbing Joanna awkwardly from Erika's arms, I held her head up with one hand while sticking the other one awkwardly under her crotch so she wouldn't slip out from under my arms.

She was heavier than I'd imagined. I prayed she wouldn't start crying, but she remained quiet, still clutching the pink squeaky doll, her head back, gazing at me. No instant, intense feeling of parental love, no epiphanies. We were two strangers meeting for the first time, one deathly afraid of dropping the other. I tentatively pressed my nose into her wispy blond hair and smelled a hint of baby powder and lotion.

After a couple of minutes that felt like an hour, Erika took Joanna back from me and sat her on the floor to test her motor skills, but she toppled right over. She propped Joanna up on all fours, but the moment she let go, Joanna collapsed onto her belly and cried. Erika picked her up, held her close and kissed her, reassuring her quietly like a natural mother.

Joanna was very weak, just as we'd heard from the Polish neurologist months earlier. But other than her motor skills she looked better than I'd expected. She couldn't possibly be disabled. It had to be the lack of stimulation in the orphanage, as the doctor had told us on our conference call. She just needed two devoted, loving parents to take care of her.

Joanna began to wriggle in Erika's arms, a sour expression on her face. She needed another diaper change. Erika said something to the white-haired woman, who nodded in response.

"Honey, I'm going to change her diaper. I'll be right back." She followed the white-haired woman as Joanna glanced over her shoulder at me. I smiled and waved to her as she disappeared out the door.

I wouldn't see her again until tomorrow, when our journey together would begin, and wished I could tell her that this would be her last night alone; we weren't leaving her behind.

*Just wait till morning and we'll be back. I promise.*

Standing in the middle of the room, I glanced around at Renata, Danuta, and Karina. They looked at me, smiling, as I tried to take in everything I'd seen, heard, and felt over the last hour. We couldn't communicate but I sensed by their reassuring looks that these women were trying to tell me that everything would be okay. We were making the right choice. Joanna would be fine.

I let out a long puff of air, collecting my thoughts. Even if I'd spoken the language, I didn't think I could've put words to what I was feeling. Maybe it'd take a while to sink in. I was hot and my limbs felt like Jell-O as Erika rejoined us. Renata broke the silence, motioning us toward the door. "We need to go back to hotel. Marian is outside with car. We come back tomorrow."

———

At eight o'clock the next morning we were back at the orphanage to pick up Joanna for the long trip back to Warsaw, which we would embark on after spending the night at the local tourist hotel, the Hotel Orbis. Renata sorted out the paperwork that granted us temporary custody as Joanna's legal guardians with the orphanage director

We would officially become her parents after we went to court in a few days, assuming, of course, that the court approved of us as parents. Then we could get Joanna's medical exam and apply to the American embassy for her visa to enter the United States. Renata assured us that there would be no problems. I prayed she was right.

Erika dressed Joanna in clothes we'd brought—a pink jumper, lacy ankle socks, and a blue-striped sunbonnet. It was a complete transformation. She became a dazzling little girl. Danuta, Karina, and the white-haired woman walked us back through the foyer to the front door. Renata and Marian walked ahead to the car. The women had tears in their eyes.

There was no doubt that Joanna was special to them. They'd miss her deeply. Each of them smothered her with hugs and kisses. One of them said, *"Kocham cię,"* Polish for "I love you." Erika, tearing up, said something I couldn't understand and hugged both women.

I swallowed hard. "Honey, please tell them for me she'll be okay. She'll have a great life and be safe with us."

"That's what I just told them." She wiped her eyes.

I bowed to them with my hands together in a gesture of thanks. *Dziękuję.* They nodded and waved. This was the Hall-mark moment I'd been waiting for.

We called out *"Do widzenia"*—"Goodbye"—before squeezing back into the little Nissan. Without an infant seat, I held Joanna tightly on my lap behind Renata. She was still quiet and emotionless. Erika slid in next to me behind Marian.

"Do you want me to hold her?"

"No, I want to hold her. Then you can hold her for a while. We'll take turns." Erika laughed and punched my arm. We were like two kids fighting over a new puppy.

As Marian pulled away, Erika and I watched the beige stucco building with the red tile roof recede behind us. The tall, skinny boy stood alone on the terrace watching us. This time he wasn't smiling. Across the street from the orphanage, the green waters of Lake Juno peeked through the trees, a man and woman barely visible paddling by in a canoe. A little blue Russian GAZ mail truck sputtered by, belching diesel smoke. It was another hot but beautiful summer day in Mrągowo.

I pulled off Joanna's sunbonnet and kissed her head. "Hi, sweetie. It's Daddy and that's Mommy. You're gonna be okay now. You're coming home with us. You'll never be alone again."

She looked up at me with the same blank expression, then craned her neck so that she could peer out the rear window at the orphanage and caretakers receding into the distance.

# FIVE

We'd reserved a double room at the Hotel Forum Warszawa, which catered to European tourists. As far as I could tell, we were the only Americans there.

We parted with Renata and Marian at the hotel entrance, then walked through the lobby with Joanna, who was slumped over asleep in our collapsible stroller. A well-dressed, officious young man and woman with the charm of the Motor Vehicles Department stood behind the front desk watching as we crossed to the elevator banks.

When we left the hotel the day before we were childless; now we had a baby in a stroller. Did they suspect we were American baby snatchers on a poaching trip to Poland? Would they report us to the authorities?

As we stood waiting for the elevator, I made sidelong glances to see if they were still watching us, but they'd turned back to their computer screens. Perhaps I was just paranoid. Erika stood next to me, one hand on the stroller, her hair frizzed and her skin glowing from the heat.

Looking down at Joanna slumped in the stroller, I couldn't get over how impossibly adorable she looked with a simple change into girly clothes. I crouched down next to her and put my nose up to her mouth. Erika watched me, puzzled.

"What are you doing?" she asked.

I smiled up at her. "Making sure she's still breathing. She's so quiet."

Erika rolled her eyes. I hoisted myself back up. "She was really easy in the car ride on the way back, wasn't she? Hardly made a peep."

"Yup."

As if trying to reassure myself that everything was under control now that we were together, I continued. "I think the hard part is behind us now that we've got her. I'll be a mighty happy dad if she keeps snoozing away like this."

"Don't bet on it," Erika said. "Babies are a *lot* of work." The elevator door opened and we maneuvered the stroller with our precious charge into the car.

I shrugged off Erika's warning. "Now *you're* the worrywart."

Once we'd stepped into our room and let the door shut, we sighed with relief; we were finally alone together. Joanna opened her eyes and straightened up in her stroller. I crouched down to eye level with her.

"Hi there. Have a good nap?"

She glowered at me and writhed around in the stroller. Thankfully, Erika's motherly instincts kicked in. She unbuckled Joanna, lifted her out of the stroller, and set her down on one of the twin beds we'd pushed together, but she toppled over.

We propped her up with pillows and emptied our cache of toys onto the beds, hoping she'd occupy herself with her new playthings—plastic blocks, books made of cloth, a sterling silver rattle, stuffed animals, a rubber ball—but she started to cry. Looking at Erika, I froze. "Oh God. Baby crying. What do we do?" I'd fantasized for months about being the perfect dad, but now I felt completely useless.

Erika picked her up from the bed and whispered to her while gently bouncing her up and down. The bouncing seemed to distract her and she stopped crying.

There wasn't a lot of space to walk around our room, but after a week in Poland we were used to everything being cramped. Because there was only a tiny closet and dresser, our suitcases were spread all over the floor. Joanna's hotel crib was crammed between our beds and the wall, leaving a little pathway to the bathroom.

I was relieved that at least one of us had some natural parenting instincts. It certainly wasn't me. "How did you know what to do?"

"I took care of my brother Richard when he was a baby and I was ten. I loved it until he threw up all over me."

Erika grew weary from the bouncing. Joanna coughed up phlegm from her cold. She looked miserable and I didn't dare touch her. Maybe we needed a doctor, but how would we find one late at night in Warsaw? Erika put Joanna back down.

"Let me check her diaper." I felt like an idiot, like when my car wouldn't start and all I could think of was to check the oil, as if that would help.

Erika put a fresh diaper on her, replacing the old-fashioned pinned cloth diaper with something convenient and disposable—a Pamper. Joanna quieted down for a minute but then started back up again. I watched helplessly, feeling my headache coming back from her squealing. I prayed that the people in the room next door couldn't hear us through the thick cinder-block walls. Standing in the pathway carved out in front of our beds, I felt powerless. "What do we do now?"

Erika remained calm. "She's probably hungry."

"Right. Good idea." I felt like we were in a Three Stooges movie where they suddenly found themselves in charge of a baby.

The orphanage staff had given us several old-fashioned glass bottles full of soup, formula, and other liquefied food. Joanna was fed from a bottle even though a fourteen-month-old should have been eating solid foods from a spoon. Erika lifted her from our beds, shushing her while grabbing the bottle of lukewarm carrot soup, sticking the rubber nipple into Joanna's mouth. It worked. She quieted down and sucked away. Thank God for women when it came to caring for a baby in a foreign hotel room. I made a mental note: *When the baby cries, hold her and bounce her around. If she's still crying, check diaper. If she just won't shut up, feed her.* I could remember that.

Once Joanna quieted down I could think again. My attention turned to the two bottles of liquid food left on the dresser. "Uh, honey, what do we do when those two bottles are empty?" Erika looked at me, impatient. "We find a supermarket and get her baby food that she can take from a bottle."

Shooting me a look of feigned superiority, she smiled mischievously. "Here, Mr. Mom. You can feed her now." She handed Joanna to me with the bottle sticking out of her mouth. "I have to go to the bathroom."

I'd never fed a baby before and felt like I'd been given a ticking hand grenade. I cradled her awkwardly in the crook of my arm, trying not to drop the bottle. She had a blissful look on her face, eyes half shut as she finished. I took the bottle from her and looked for something to wipe her mouth with, finally using my shirttail. She gazed at me, just as she had in the orphanage the day before. *Now what do I do?* Erika was still in the bathroom.

I walked her over to the window. We had an expansive view

of a drab, gray, sprawling city. A faint pinkish red sunset was filtered through a thin layer of smog. Across the street was one of the tallest and perhaps ugliest buildings in Europe, the Palace of Culture and Science. Built in the fifties, it was a "gift" from the Soviet Union.

Joanna looked out at the view, seemingly mesmerized by the flow of traffic down below, a bustling swarm of small cars and trucks that must have looked like toys to her. Erika returned from the bathroom looking weary but happy. "Did you remember to burp her?"

"Burp her?" I remembered reading about it in a baby book somewhere. Erika rolled her eyes as she took Joanna from me, hoisting her over her shoulder. "You always burp a baby after she eats." Another mental note: *Reread chapter in baby book about burping the baby.*

I called room service to order sandwiches, beer, and hot water for making baby formula, and then flipped through the channels on the TV: a Russian game show, German news, Italian soccer, French political talk show, Polish documentary on Hitler, CNN. Thank God, something I could understand.

Erika buckled Joanna back into her stroller and parked her three feet from the TV. She stared at the screen, unblinking, apparently hypnotized by the wonders of television and the news of the world. I collapsed on the hard beds, spent, as a breaking story came on about Boris Yeltsin, the first elected president of Russia. "How long have we been at this parenting now? Four hours? I'm exhausted. I don't know how I'm going to get through this for another eighteen years."

Erika plopped down next to me. "Get used to it."

My eyes fixated on Joanna in the stroller in front of the flickering light. Here we were watching TV together like a real family.

"Just kidding. I meant to say it was a *good* exhausted. I'm loving every minute of it."

By the time room service arrived with our dinner and we ate, it was close to ten o'clock. Joanna was still awake in front of the TV, squirming in her stroller. "Let's put her to bed." Erika unsnapped her from the stroller, checked her diaper, and laid her in the crib on her belly with a wool blanket, the pink squeaky doll, a stuffed bunny, and a goose-down comfort pillow she'd bought at a gift shop in Warsaw.

Joanna kicked and thrashed like a turtle trying to right itself, then pulled herself up into a crouched position on her hands and knees. Letting out a soft hum, she rocked back and forth on her knees while staring straight ahead. Erika and I watched, transfixed, through the bars of the crib. She seemed to have no awareness that we were there. Erika whispered, "Oh my God. I think she's trying to rock herself to sleep." I studied her. "Wow. We saw those kids on TV, in the Romanian orphanages, do the same thing."

She was referring to an ABC News *20/20* exposé we'd seen the year before about Romanian children abandoned in state orphanages, the disastrous result of a bizarre plan concocted by the Ceaușescu dictatorship to force women to bear children for the state. The televised images were heartbreaking—youngsters in straitjackets confined to metal bed frames in bleak, cold rooms; mentally disturbed adolescents left alone in silence, rocking back and forth; neglected infants drowning in their own filth, too weak to cry.

After about ten minutes, Joanna collapsed in a heap, crying. Maybe it was her rattly cough that kept her from sleeping. Erika jumped out of bed, picked her up, bouncing and shushing her, but Joanna's distress seemed to get worse. Her crying became an ear-piercing scream.

I'd never heard such a desperate wail. Didn't she have an *off* switch somewhere? We'd had a long day and needed sleep. Erika kept bouncing her up and down, rocking her back and forth. She sat her by the TV, but Joanna wouldn't settle down.

An hour later, at eleven o'clock, Joanna finally calmed herself. Erika laid her back down on her stomach in the crib, kissed her hot sweaty head, and covered her with the wool blanket, pulling the comfort pillow up close to her face.

We looked at each other, exhausted. I felt like we were two bomb disposal experts who'd just defused an improvised explosive device. Looking over the bar of the crib, careful not to disturb her, I listened to her breathe. Her nose was stuffy, so she breathed through her mouth, wheezing from the congestion in her chest. I whispered to her, "Poor kid. You won't be alone at night anymore."

Then I blew her a kiss good night.

# SIX

Two days after returning from Mrągowo, we sat in court for our adoption hearing. Since we could not bring Joanna, our hotel had recommended a girl who appeared to be about fifteen or sixteen to watch her in our room. We weren't thrilled at the notion of our first separation from Joanna, even for a couple of hours, but we had little choice. Erika gave the young sitter a brief interview in Polish and determined that she was trustworthy.

The courtroom was small but ornate. The raised bench, desks, gallery, and carved paneling were made of mahogany. All the court officials—the judge, the state attorney, and Renata—were dressed in black robes with white silk scarves that looked like bow ties; all they needed were white powdered wigs. The only other people in the courtroom were two jurors, a court reporter, and a translator for me, the only non-Polish-speaker in the room.

The atmosphere was solemn. Erika and I sat behind a long table, facing the judge and jurors. It felt as though everyone's eyes were trained on us, except for the judge, who was busy looking at our file, talking with Renata and the state attorney. I tried to read their facial cues and vocal tones to get a sense of where the hearing may lead us. With only a vague understanding of the Polish judiciary, we had to take Renata's word that all would be fine. I prayed that she was correct.

My palms were cold and sweaty. Erika grabbed my hand for moral support. I surveyed the room for anyone who looked kind or supportive, but all I saw were stern, almost blank expressions that revealed nothing. If it weren't for Renata and Erika sitting next to me, I would've felt even more helpless than I did.

The judge called the court to order. She looked to be in her forties, very professional and commanding. Maybe she was a mother herself. If so, perhaps she'd warm up to us and be sympathetic to our case. At the very least she'd be impressed by Erika's Polish. But the judge had a grave look on her face as she spoke. The translator whispered to me that she was outlining the facts of the case. The judge turned toward me and spoke. I leaned toward the translator.

"The judge wants you to take witness stand," she said.

Erika squeezed my hand hard as I stood up. "Don't forget to breathe."

My mind raced and my mouth felt thick as if full of sand as I faced the judge, feeling more like an accused criminal than an adoptive-parent-to-be. The judge glanced up at me and then read from a document I couldn't understand. The translator was nearly a foot shorter than I was, so I bent down to listen to her translation. "She is introducing you to court," she said.

The judge directed something to me that sounded like a question. The translator whispered, "What are your feelings for this child?"

The judge looked at me with an impassive expression. I froze, my head a swirl of thoughts. We'd literally just met Joanna but we weren't about to let anyone take her away from us. Yet to her, we were strangers. Should I lie? Would it have jeopardized the entire hearing if I did? I should have thought this through beforehand.

It felt as if an hour had passed while the judge waited for my response before I blurted out to the translator, "I am absolutely in love with this child. I already feel bonded to her."

*God, that was so stupid.*

The judge squinted at the translator and asked another question. "Do you understand that this child will have the same rights as if it were your biological child?"

I swallowed and nodded. "Yes, Your Honor." *Please like me.*

Another question. I bent down to listen to the translator. "Do you agree that you are undertaking a lifelong commitment to care for and raise this child?"

*Of course I do, if you'll just let us adopt her!*

"Yes, Your Honor."

*"Dziękuję. Proszę siedzieć."* The translator said that the judge thanked me and asked that I sit down. I bowed respectfully to the judge and did as I was instructed. Then Erika took the witness stand and breezed through all the questions in Polish.

*Show-off.*

The judge asked for a twenty-minute recess. Erika and I stepped into the lobby outside the courtroom while Renata stayed inside. We were alone in the cavernous hall, silent except for the echo of occasional footsteps. I was exhausted even though the hearing itself had lasted only minutes. We gave each other a long hug, saying nothing.

I paced back and forth, my hands jammed in my pockets, imagining the worst. There would be a problem. Maybe our paperwork was incomplete. Maybe a directive from a government minister had shut down all foreign adoptions. Joanna would have to be sent back to the orphanage and we'd be sent home.

There was a click of heels behind us on the marble floor bouncing off the high ceiling—Renata. She smiled and waved for us to come back. "It is very good," she said.

I felt light-headed as we followed her back into the court-room. More stern faces. The judge asked Erika and me to stand; Renata joined us. I bent down to listen to the translator read the verdict in English as the judge addressed the court.

"In the case submitted by John R. Brooks and Erika Brooks, née Borkowski, both citizens of the USA, to adopt the minor Polish citizen Joanna Dymowska, the court decides to: (1) decree the adoption of the child to the Brookses, (2) give the child the surname "Brooks," (3) change the first name to "Casey," and (4) prepare a new Certificate of Birth."

The judge looked up from the document and smiled warmly at us for the first time.

"*Gratulacje, Pan i Pani Brooks!*" Congratulations, Mr. and Mrs. Brooks! I was in disbelief. Did this just happen? The atmosphere in the courtroom instantly shifted from somber to joyous. Everyone broke into smiles and nods of support. Erika and I grabbed each other and Renata in a bear hug.

Joanna Dymowska was now officially Casey Joanna Brooks, and we were legally her parents in the eyes of the Polish court.

# SEVEN

With the court hearing behind us, we were off with Renata to see a Polish pediatric neurologist for Casey's medical exam. With the neurologist's seal of approval, we could clear the American embassy for Casey's visa and be home free. We'd come so far in such a short time; I could almost see the finish line. But the process turned out to be more than just a formality.

In 1987, the Reagan administration made it illegal for people with AIDS to enter the United States. Further, after the horror stories from Romanian orphanages, the State Department clamped down on health standards for foreigners applying for a U.S. visa. If a qualified Polish physician refused to certify to the U.S. embassy that Casey was healthy, according to broad State Department guidelines that seemed to go far beyond AIDS, we couldn't bring her home with us.

Renata told us that the embassy referred many of its visa applicants to this doctor. She wasn't particularly warm, but the embassy trusted her and Renata had never had an issue with her in other adoption cases. She'd be on our side.

Her office was in an elegant nineteenth-century building—one of the few in Warsaw not leveled in the war—on a tree-lined street in an upscale neighborhood. Erika, Renata, and I sat quietly in the waiting room, Renata fidgeting with a cigarette while Erika pushed Casey back and forth in her stroller. Casey soothed herself by rubbing the tip of her nose until it was red and chapped, apparently a habit she'd taught herself in the orphanage, where the children weren't allowed pacifiers because of concerns about germs.

It had been less than a week since we'd left the orphanage, and Casey had made astounding progress from the quiet, lethargic infant we'd first met. She was more alert, expressive, cheery, and chatty with us, even though her vocabulary consisted of grunts, shrieks, and bursts of *bahs* and *dahs*.

She banged around with the toys we brought and had become fixated on MTV, one of three English-language cable channels in our hotel room. Best of all, with a pillow for support, she could sit up by herself. She was still prone to irritability and screaming fits, especially around bedtime, but that was probably to be expected of a fourteen-month-old.

The door to the doctor's office opened and a woman in a white lab coat stepped out. She appeared to be in her fifties, short and wide in stature, with a stern face. She held up a pair of reading glasses slung around her neck, squinting at a clipboard in her hand. "Brooks?" She looked up at us, unexpressive, and motioned for us to follow her into her office.

For the next twenty minutes I watched, bewildered, as she sat Casey on a stainless-steel examination table. Though her strength and balance had improved, she was still tipsy sitting up without support. The doctor looked into her eyes, ears, and throat, and listened to her lungs with a stethoscope. She tested her for a parachute reflex, holding her up on all fours, but she collapsed on the table. The doctor scowled. She tested for hand-eye coordination and pincer skills, and tapped her elbows and knees with a rubber-tipped reflex-testing hammer.

Everyone spoke in agitated voices. Renata hovered over the doctor and gesticulated, talking excitedly. The doctor, still expressionless, said something to Erika; she shook her head no. Casey began to fuss. The doctor made notes on her clipboard, a hard look on her face. My pulse quickened. This didn't look good. If only the doctor had seen how much Casey had improved since we'd left the orphanage.

Renata scowled, looking irritated. She spoke to the doctor in a stern voice, waving her arms up and down, pointing to Casey. The doctor listened impassively but shook her head. Erika had a worried look on her face. Renata asked us to wait outside the office with Casey while she finished her business with the neurologist. Once out in the hallway, I was desperate for information. "Honey, what the hell is going on?"

Erika let out a long sigh. "The doctor's concerned about Casey's development and motor skills, like the fact that she didn't react to the parachute test and is still tipsy sitting up."

I grimaced.

"She said that Casey really should be walking right now. She even said something about Casey's head being a bit flat."

"What? Are you kidding? I thought that was an old wives' tale." Erika once told me about the Poles' fixation on round-headed babies—anything less than a head the shape of a basketball was considered unattractive.

I shook my head in disbelief. "So she thinks Casey's head is unattractive, as if that means anything."

Erika rolled her eyes and shrugged. After a few minutes, Renata joined us in the hallway, looking defeated as she lit another cigarette. We waited as she inhaled deeply, blowing the smoke up to the ceiling, shaking her head. My heart sank. Wasn't this supposed to be a formality? Renata coughed and waved the smoke away from her face. "She say she cannot certify to U.S. embassy that Joanna is healthy, so we cannot get visa."

We stood in the hallway, dazed, absorbing the weight of Renata's bombshell. All three of us were quiet as Casey sat in her stroller chewing on a multicolored cloth starfish. My mind went into free fall.

Though Casey was now legally our child under Polish law, according to international law, Erika and I were American citizens in Poland on a temporary tourist visa. Casey was a Polish citizen with no exit visa. We couldn't take her home until her visa problem was resolved, and we could stay together in Poland for only a limited time, until *our* visas expired. I had outlandish thoughts of us overstaying, but we could risk deportation, jail time, or, worst of all, losing Casey.

We turned again to Renata.

She put out her cigarette. "Look, this should not be problem if we get second opinion from other doctor."

Erika and I brightened as Casey used the cloth starfish to rub her nose.

"Really?" I asked tentatively.

"I make appointment for second opinion at children's hospital tomorrow," Renata said with an air of confidence. "It will be okay. I know director there."

She never ceased to amaze me.

———

The next day, Erika, Casey, and I took a taxi to the Warszawski Szpital dla Dzieci, the Warsaw Children's Hospital, where we were to meet with a child psychologist for a second opinion. Renata couldn't be there with us, but she calmed our fears of going alone, assuring us that this exam would go smoothly. We had no choice but to trust her. So far, she'd successfully navigated us through a series of hurdles and setbacks. This was the last one.

We pulled up to an imposing building that was nearly a block long. Built in the 1700s, it hadn't aged gracefully. The forbidding façade looked like it hadn't been cleaned in decades. Black flags hung from the windows. What the hell were they for? Weren't black flags a symbol of mourning? I wished we'd insisted that Renata come with us.

We left the taxi and walked into the main reception area, Erika wheeling Casey in the collapsible stroller. She was dressed in her sunbonnet, a frilly top with matching pants, and white booties, looking every bit like a kewpie doll, her hand clamped on the pink squeaky doll we'd given her at the orphanage. The lights in the reception area were turned off and there was little activity where normally we would've expected to see a traffic jam of people. I turned to Erika. "Did you notice those black flags out front?"

She looked spooked. "How could I miss them? I wonder what they're for?"

We found a young woman sitting behind a desk and approached her for help. I listened helplessly as Erika and the woman exchanged incomprehensible chatter before she pointed us toward the elevator. As we made our way across the reception area, the eerie silence around me became increasingly disconcerting. While waiting for the elevator, I leaned toward Erika. "What were you guys talking about?"

"I asked what the black flags were outside."

"Yeah?"

"She said the staff is on strike because the hospital lacks medicine. The state is having trouble paying salaries and they've had to shut down some services."

*Perfect.*

We squeezed into a rickety cage about the size of a phone booth that looked like it had gone into service in the nineteenth century. I pushed the black accordion gate shut and hit the button for the fifth floor. The car jolted upward past floors that were dark and lifeless.

My fear of confined spaces gripped me, particularly cramped elevators. Ever since an episode in a lower Manhattan loft in 1985 when I was stuck in a crowded, steamy service elevator for an hour, I had dreaded confinement of any sort. I scanned the top of the car for an escape route—my way of calming my fears. Perspiration ran down my back. "I don't know about you guys, but I think I'll take the stairs down." Erika put her hand on my arm. "C'mon, honey. Breathe. We're almost there."

The car came to an abrupt stop on the fifth floor. I jerked the gate open, relieved that it hadn't gotten stuck and trapped us. I didn't want my daughter to freak out watching her claustrophobic dad in the middle of a panic attack.

We stepped into a darkened, dingy hallway. It looked abandoned and had the stale smell so typical of Soviet-era buildings, something akin to the acrid scent of an electrical fire. A cluster of beds, wheelchairs, walkers, and food carts had been pushed to one side of the hallway, leaving the other side open to foot traffic, but there was only us.

We walked down the hallway, peering cautiously into each office, looking for signs of life, but every room we passed was empty. I was disturbed. "I really think we should've waited until Renata could be with us. This place looks like it's out of business."

At the last door in the hallway, Erika knocked softly and opened it. Looking inside, we found an attractive young woman in a white lab coat writing at a green metal desk. She looked to be barely out of medical school. I whispered to Erika, "Maybe she speaks English."

Erika approached her. *"Przepraszam, czy Panienka, mowi po angielsku?"* Excuse me, madam, do you speak English?

The woman looked up, annoyed, and answered. "Yes, and you are?"

"John and Erika Brooks. We're looking for the child psychologist. Our lawyer, Renata, said she'd made an appointment with the psychologist to examine our daughter."

The young woman perked up and stood to greet us. "Of course. I'm the psychologist." She extended Casey her finger. "And who is this?" Casey grabbed it and the woman shook it. Casey smiled.

"This is our daughter, Casey," Erika said. "You may know that the embassy doctor wanted a second opinion before she was willing to sign off on Casey's medical certificate for her visa."

"Yes, certainly." The psychologist pointed us toward the examination room. "Please. I'll be there in just a moment."

We stepped into a small, dark room. A sour smell permeated the air from a puddle of yellow liquid on the metal examination table. I tapped Erika on the shoulder. "Honey, look at this. Is this what I think it is?"

Erika put her nose up to it and jerked back. "It's urine!"

The psychologist walked in, noticing our reaction to the mess. "I'm so sorry. We had another patient here with a bladder problem. It hasn't been cleaned up yet. We are short on help because of the strike." We turned our backs on the examination table while the young woman unbuckled Casey from the stroller and picked her up.

We spent about a half hour together. Erika told the psychologist Casey's story, with particular emphasis on the encouraging opinion we'd received in April from the Polish neurologist and Casey's dramatic progress in just a week. The psychologist nodded as she listened to Erika.

We watched anxiously as the psychologist put Casey through the same series of tests that the other doctor had performed the day before—sitting up, parachute reflex, tweezer skills, cognitive abilities. She was still weak and couldn't complete a number of tasks. After a while Casey became cranky and started to cry. The psychologist purred at her as she handed her back to Erika.

We were quiet as we watched the young woman, her back to us, jotting down notes in a spiral binder. She turned around in her chair to face us. "She doesn't seem to be able to perform all of the tasks that a child this age should perform." Erika and I stared at her, nodding vacantly. "So I can understand the other doctor's concerns, but I think she is just weak from inactivity." We broke into smiles. I felt a weight lifting.

"And it's a good sign that she's improved so quickly in the past few days." Erika and I nodded excitedly at her like a couple of bobbleheads.

*Thank you! Thank you!*

Wrapping up the examination, the psychologist said, "I will give the neurologist my observations. That should be sufficient for your daughter's U.S. visa requirement. Good luck."

I wanted to kiss this woman. *"Dziękuję! Dziękuję!"*

*"Nie ma za co."* You're welcome. She smiled. "Your Polish is very good."

Hallelujah. Home free.

Having exhausted my vacation days from work, I returned home to Connecticut. Erika remained with Casey for another two weeks as guests of her aunt Nusia and uncle Marian in Wrocław until Casey's U.S. visa was issued.

# EIGHT

Over the next few years, Erika and I eased into traditional parenting roles. With the adoption ordeal behind us, we wanted to settle down to a normal family life, and for the most part it was. I went to work at a small investment firm, while Erika gave up her jewelry business to stay home with Casey. We agreed that she needed a full-time parent after everything she'd been through.

From the very beginning, we told Casey about her adoption, but since we knew almost nothing about her birth family, we resorted to a scripted fantasy story.

*Your mother loved you very much but she was poor and couldn't care for you. She wanted you to have a better life than she could provide. Mommy and I went all the way to Poland to find you because God meant for us to be together as a family.*

Casey never showed much curiosity during these conversations. She never asked about her birth mother, whether she had siblings or who her birth father could have been. Much to Erika's dismay, she had little interest in Polish culture, never watched the hours of video I'd shot during our trip, and when asked if she wanted to meet her birth mother someday waved us off, annoyed. So we took her at her word, leaving the door open to talk and hoping someday she'd come around.

As time passed, the orphanage became a distant memory. I'd hoped it had been completely erased from Casey's consciousness. She was a member of our family now—no different from a biological child in our minds—so we taught her our ancestral narratives. I even tried to convince her that she looked just like my mother as a young girl. After all, they both had round faces, fair complexions, and light hair cut pageboy style; they looked the same to me. But in truth, I had no idea how our words resonated in her sharp little mind.

By the time she was two, Casey had caught up to her age group. She was no longer the quiet, withdrawn child we'd met at the orphanage, but a happy, affectionate, bright little girl. She'd sprouted a pearly white head of hair, so fine and silky that it tangled easily. We took great care to comb out the knots without pulling out chunks of hair. Her almond-shaped eyes turned from blue to a greenish hazel brown, and every time she smiled her dimples lit up.

She tottered around the house like a penguin and developed a surprisingly sophisticated vocabulary, skipping over much of the baby talk for more or less complete sentences. She had a high voice with a hint of a lisp from being born with a high palate; it made her sound like Elmer Fudd. *Look* was "wook," *crying* was "cwying," *birthday* was "buwfday," and *Santa* was "Thanta." She had the kind of laugh you wanted to store away in your memory forever—mouth-wide-open, full-throated, pure joy, straight from the belly: *Ha ha ha!* It was delicious to hear.

We stocked her early years with as much happiness as we

could, enrolling her in preschool, making playdates, and spending nearly every weekend on some kind of adventure. On blistering summer days we cooled off at the local swimming hole. In the fall we trudged up Talcott Mountain to show her the display of color in the valley below. Winter was for sledding, snow forts, and trips to see Santa at the mall.

In 1995, we moved from Simsbury to San Francisco so that I could take a job as chief financial officer of a radio group. Our new neighborhood in Marin County, just over the Golden Gate Bridge, teemed with kids, and before long Casey had a gaggle of new friends. They started kindergarten and stuck together through grade school. We joined a church, St. Stephen's Episcopal in Belvedere, and put Casey in Sunday school. Everyone was welcoming and friendly and it didn't take long for us to fall in love with the place.

Our early years in California were a time of discovery for her. Casey was a natural ham who loved the theater. When she was six, she was onstage at the Playhouse in San Anselmo singing "Give My Regards to Broadway" with her musical theater group. She was a devoted foodie, chowing down on barbecued oysters in Bodega Bay, mussels in Santa Cruz, sushi at Pier 39, and dim sum in Chinatown. As she made her way through grade school, she racked up an impressive collection of accolades from her teachers:

*A joy to have in class!*
*So thoughtful and well behaved!*
*Spunky and spirited!*

Casey's teachers told us that she was the one who'd seek out and welcome the new kid in class. She was the one who'd sit with the girl who was alone. She was the one to make peace amid a feud.

By the time she was eight, like most girls her age, Casey had one foot planted firmly in childhood innocence while the other ventured into preteen pursuits. Her room was home to a massive collection of Beanie Babies, Lego pieces, an unfinished dollhouse, piles of dirty clothes, and a pet rat named Banjo. Her comfort pillow from Poland was never far away. It was all so normal.

She devoured the books that all the kids loved—*Harry Potter*, *The Lord of the Rings*, *The Chronicles of Narnia*. But video games usually won out for her attention—Super Mario, Yoshi, and Sim-City. She and her friends sat mesmerized in front of the TV, their hands and fingers twisting, turning and jabbing at their remotes. Her musical tastes ran from Britney Spears and the Spice Girls to the Backstreet Boys, the pop stars of the time. She was obsessed with her appearance, her outfits displaying a unique and eclectic style. A typical morning would have found her running out the door in a school sweatshirt over jeans, purple socks, and blue Converse sneakers with multicolored laces, just another kid trying to carve out an identity without alienating the pack.

She lugged around a purple JanSport backpack jangling with colorful adornments like a Christmas tree. There was a pink pig, a soccer ball, a tiny blue-on-white New York license plate inscribed CASEY, and a whistle that Erika had insisted on, just in case of emergency. Most important were her Pokémon cards—Charmander, Squirtle, Jigglypuff, and everyone's favorite—the cute, yellow, mousy Pikachu. She traded them with her friend Rebecca during lunch.

———

Still, Casey had her unsettling moments. In one of her first letters to me from Poland, after I'd returned to the States ahead of her, Erika reported that Casey had recoiled at the feel of grass. During their stay in Wrocław waiting for Casey's visa, they relaxed in Uncle

Marian's small but beautifully manicured backyard, soft and lush like a pint-size golf course with a flower and vegetable garden. But when Erika set Casey down on the grass she'd cried hysterically to be picked up. I'd read that preemies like Casey had very sensitive skin. Some could only tolerate ultrasoft fabrics because wools and polyesters were too scratchy. Perhaps that was it.

There were more episodes of tantrums and meltdowns like the one we'd seen during our first night together in the Hotel Forum in Warsaw. Something trivial, like waiting an extra minute for ice cream or leaving Toys "R" Us just a moment too soon, could send Casey into a fit of screaming, thrashing, and flailing about. Just getting her to calm down for bedtime often left us feeling as we did that first night in Warsaw—like bomb disposal experts.

———

She refused to yield to authority at home without a fight, and had to be in control. Simple requests to clean up her room, put her dishes in the dishwasher, turn off the TV, or do her homework often triggered howls of protest. We had flare-ups at the mall, flares-ups in restaurants, flare-ups in front of the grandparents. Sometimes I couldn't stop myself from spanking her, feeling horribly ashamed of myself later.

It wasn't so much the frequency of these flare-ups—a week could pass with Casey on her best behavior—it was their intensity. Her rages seemed to stem from an almost bottomless well of anguish for which there seemed no comfort other than to cry it out.

We felt powerless to soothe her or protect her from herself. It was as if she deliberately pushed us away. And when we complied, she panicked at the prospect of being left behind. Still, she'd shove everything and everyone aside so that she could deal with her emotions and process her setbacks on her own. That was her coping system.

I'd never seen such a toxic mixture of anger and despair in a three-year-old girl and I felt helpless to repair it.

Years later, around Christmastime, when Casey was eight, she begged us to take her ice-skating with her friend Tessa at the Yerba Buena skating rink in San Francisco. She was in a festive mood, sporting a red stocking cap with a fuzzy pom-pom that made her look like a merry elf.

After Erika and I got the girls into their skates, they stepped gingerly onto the ice, holding hands. Casey had been on skates only once before.

Unsteady on her feet, she clung to Tessa for support like Bambi trying to stand on all four legs on the icy pond. Erika and I cringed as we watched her.

Within minutes, Casey's skates flew out from under her. She fell backward and hit her head on the ice—not hard, but she yanked off her stocking cap and grabbed her head, crying inconsolably while she lay in the middle of the rink, skaters twirling around her. Tessa extended her hand but Casey swatted it away and curled into a ball, shielding herself so the crowd wouldn't see that her face was beet red. Erika rushed to her side and tried to pick her up.

"Get away from me!" she screamed. "Why did you make me come here? I hate you!" The crowd closed in. Tessa was in tears. I got on my knees to talk to her, almost in a whisper. "C'mon, honey. You need to get up. Please? It's okay. Let's just go home. You'll be all right." Casey slowly picked herself up, batting my hand away with a scowl, too proud to accept help as she hobbled off the ice. She must have been humiliated and angry at herself for making such a scene, and jealous that Tessa had mastered what she couldn't.

After dropping Tessa off, we pulled into our driveway. Casey sat buckled into her seat sulking, ignoring us. Erika and I got out of the car and walked up to the front door. Erika stepped inside while I stood at the front door waiting for her.

"C'mon, honey. C'mon inside." I stood a minute longer, watching her, but she wouldn't look at me. I knew if I went back to get her she'd just wave me off.

"Okay, I'm going inside."

Moments later, Erika and I stood in the kitchen, silent, deflated. We heard a faint sound coming from Casey's bedroom. She'd apparently snuck into the house and gone straight to her room, where she sobbed quietly. We tiptoed up to the door and peeked in.

She lay facedown on her bed with her red parka on, her face buried in her sheets, her silky hair a knotted mess. I watched from the door as Erika sat next to her on the bed. She tried to rub her back, but Casey put her arm up to keep her mother from touching her.

"Honey, what's wrong?" Erika asked.

Casey just stared past her.

"Can I get you something?"

Casey shook her head.

"Do you want us to leave you alone?"

She nodded.

"Okay, sweetie pie. Then let me take your jacket."

Casey let Erika pull the red parka off and didn't protest when Erika rubbed her back for a minute. She kissed her on the head and we backed out of the room.

I mouthed the words *I love you* and blew her a kiss. She looked stonily ahead, patting around with her arm until it found her pillow and pulled it to her face. We shut her door behind us and the sobbing started again as she cried herself to sleep.

She seemed to have a never-ending reservoir of tears.

———

Birthdays were events that Erika and I had come to dread and prayed we'd get through without an eruption. Casey often couldn't decide whether she wanted a birthday party, even though we suspected that she secretly wanted one, but it couldn't be a surprise. She hated surprises. Perhaps on some level she felt undeserving of the attention, or was looking for a way to punish us for not loving her enough, or both. It seemed that everyone had to work extra-hard to prove their love to her.

For Christmas, once Casey had decided on her wish list—an ordeal in itself given her penchant for procrastination and indecisiveness—it had to be followed precisely. Any deviations were met with a long face and remarks such as "I didn't ask for this" or "Why didn't you get me that?" followed by trips back to the mall to exchange the offending item for cash. Not only had we failed to teach her the value of appreciation, but our attempts to make her happy on special occasions had come to nothing.

As time went on, parenting Casey often felt like breaking a wild stallion. They instinctively protect their space and dominate their handlers. Sometimes they have limited patience, lash out and bite. Only the most experienced handlers can train them. There is no single method of training that works, because every stallion is different. In each case, handlers have to project confidence and speak with authority to gain the stallion's respect. They have to be careful not to agitate or provoke it, as its natural fight-or-flight instinct could kick in, and stallions fight. In the 1998 movie *The Horse Whisperer*, Robert Redford starred as a trainer with a remarkable gift for understanding horses.

I wish I'd had a gift for understanding my own daughter.

As infuriating as her behavior was, we had no reference point to determine if this was normal, because we had no other children. Instead we'd allowed our child to manipulate us into giving her whatever she wanted in order to avert her tears. It had to be us. We were incompetent parents.

———

We searched for answers or, in their absence, reassurance. Casey's first pediatrician in Simsbury, Dr. Johnston, took a special interest in her, amazed at how she'd developed so rapidly into a lively, energetic toddler. We discussed Casey's eating and sleeping habits, how she played with other kids, how she handled transitions, and whether she followed directions. In each case, she was right in the normal range for her age.

We described the tantrums. Dr. Johnston empathized with us but couldn't see any signs of trouble. Casey would grow out of it. "Three-year-olds are still trying to get a handle on their emotions and are easily frustrated," she said, "and Casey was a preemie. They tend to be hypersensitive." I embraced Dr. Johnston's prognosis—of course Casey was fine; she'd grow out of this. She was just a strong-willed child. The subject of her abandonment and adoption was never discussed.

After our move to California, we talked to our neighborhood friend Sharon, a psychologist with a Ph.D. from Berkeley. Casey had been friends with her two kids, Ian and Caroline, since kindergarten. Ian had been adopted at birth before Sharon became pregnant with Caroline.

When I asked Sharon for her secret to good parenting, she burst out laughing. "You don't see my kids when they're at home. That's when they're at their worst. Ian can be a nightmare. He has these howling fits when he doesn't get his way." But for all the parents who assured us that their little angels were just monsters in disguise, others took a hard line.

*"You shouldn't spoil her."*

*"Be tougher with her. You have to set boundaries and stick to them."*

*"You'll only encourage her tantrums if you come to her rescue."*

Of course we'd tried time-outs and had withheld privileges such as playdates, video games, and TV. Simple chores, like making her bed and setting the table, were rewarded with gold stars on the refrigerator and treats, but this was equally unsuccessful. Disciplinary measures that worked so well with most children often pitched Casey into a fit that we feared the whole neighborhood could hear. To keep the ear-piercing decibels down, we'd cave in under the guise of *"We'll give you another chance."* The last thing we needed was a neighbor hearing the commotion from our house and calling Child Protective Services.

Erika and I tried to talk to her when she was calm, asking her why she got so angry and upset over things, what made her cry, how she felt about herself. But she'd have none of it. She felt like she was under attack, ordering us out of her room so she could be alone.

Feeling like miserable failures, Erika and I turned on each other. We came from very different parenting models. Erika's immigrant parents had always been strict and controlling, like their parents, whereas mine were fairly laid-back, like Ward and June Cleaver. Erika accused me of being too easy on Casey while I felt that Erika needed to give her a longer leash. She believed firmly—and rightly so—that we needed a united front in complete alignment against such a willful child, and she was ever watchful for any threat to the alliance.

While Casey was still in grade school, we talked to more parents, read more parenting books, taped and dissected words of wisdom from Dr. Phil. The consensus was that Casey was just a bit higher strung than the average kid, not that unusual for a girl. If we found her behavior unacceptable we just had to lay down the law with her. Eventually she'd come around.

The staff psychologist at Casey's school, Dr. Klein, repeated what we'd already heard from her teachers—good student, well-behaved, played nicely with other kids, thoughtful but sometimes a bit pushy. That was a good thing. It meant she stood up for herself. She'd never had even the mildest disciplinary citation.

We talked about Casey's early years in the orphanage, but had so little data to go on that there was no way to know what, if anything, harmful she could've inherited from her birth parents. As with our meeting years earlier with Dr. Johnston, our conference with Dr. Klein yielded little more than reassurances that lots of kids that age had coping problems; she'd grow out of it. But she didn't.

We tried therapy. In most families, it would have been ridiculous to take an eight-year-old to a shrink, but not in Marin County, where lots of kids had therapists. We thought that therapy would be a safe place where Casey might open up. Perhaps a professional would have some success drawing her out where we'd failed so miserably.

We met with a child psychologist, Dr. Darnell. She was a pleasant, soft-spoken woman in her thirties—so quiet, in fact, that she seemed almost timid. Casey could be rough around the edges when she felt threatened, so we hoped that she wouldn't make mincemeat out of Dr. Darnell.

We set up a schedule for them to meet once a week after school. But after every therapy session, Casey would come home in a churlish mood, tramp off to her room, slam the door, and dissolve into screaming fits. Dr. Darnell was "lame" and a waste of her time. They played Monopoly rather than talked and had failed to make any meaningful connection. It was difficult for us to deal with the ugly aftermath of each session. Erika and I met with Dr. Darnell for some insight over Casey's sessions, but they yielded nothing of value. Monopoly was probably not the best tool to understand our child. Between Casey's tearful pleas and belligerent protests, she ground us down, so we discontinued the sessions with Dr. Darnell.

Our break from therapy lasted less than a year. During that time much had changed in our lives. I had another new job. We'd moved from a rental to a dilapidated house the size of a shoe box we bought in the town of Tiburon, a financial stretch but an easy commute for me just over the Golden Gate Bridge from San Francisco. And after years of stalling for time, we caved in to Casey's incessant begging for a companion, adding a new member to our family. His name was Igor, a handsome, skinny, brindled English racing hound known as a whippet. They are famously gentle, sensitive, and quiet; the perfect therapy dog. Casey was in love. A family, a new job, a home, and a skinny little dog.

Things seemed to fall into place, but not quite.

# NINE

Casey had discovered a talent for writing in middle school, and I encouraged and praised her work at every opportunity. Writing was her true calling and our way to connect, just the two of us. She had a gift for vivid imagery and depth of thought well beyond her years. As she got older, her self-image became more fragile. Writing would help boost her self-confidence. One poem she'd written in eighth grade she titled "Ode to the Orange":

> *Tangy, succulent juices*
> *drip*
> *off my lips*
> *as I plunge into the first bite.*
> *It has a party*
> *in my mouth.*

But for all of her talent, Casey was a hypersensitive perfectionist. When she tried something that didn't go just right, she'd react as if her world had come to an end. She became more introverted and could no longer be coaxed onto the stage as she could in musical theater when she was younger. Shyness and self-doubt weren't unusual among preteen girls, but it complicated our attempts to introduce her to new things that could have interested her—musical instruments, chess, modern dance.

As protective as she was about her writing, she trusted me to read and edit. It was a delicate balance to be her mentor without offending her and risk turning her away from her gift or from me. I didn't want her to give up on things so easily.

Late one evening when Casey was thirteen, she was struggling with an English assignment. As I lay in bed drifting off to a *Frontline* story on PBS about Saddam Hussein and WMDs, she shuffled into our bedroom in her UGG boots, Igor trotting behind. She inched up to the bed and shoved a wrinkled mass of paper at me as though it were toxic waste. "Can you read this? I know it totally sucks."

I hated to see her beat herself up like that. "Honey, what's it about?"

"It's an essay for English on the Eiffel Tower," which came out in a rapid-fire staccato: *ItsanessayforEnglishontheEiffelTower.*

I corrected a few minor typos and punctuation errors before affixing my smiley face at the end with my verdict—*Wow!*—returning the finished piece to her as she sat at her desk. She grabbed the paper, crinkling it in her fist. I winced as I kissed the top of her head, wet from her evening shower, and left her alone to process my remarks.

Near midnight, shrieks echoed from the other side of the house—Erika and Casey at war. I had to investigate. Stepping into her room, I saw Casey at her desk, her shoulders heaving from choking sobs, while Erika stood over her with hands on hips, a disgusted look on her face. Igor lay on Casey's bed, shivering.

Erika quivered with outrage. "Why do you do this to yourself, Casey! Why!" It looked like she was on the verge of tears herself. "You're going back to therapy, young lady! I've had it!"

Casey picked her head up, tears streaming down her face. "Stop it, Mom! Therapy is stupid and useless! If you try to take me again I'll kill myself!"

*Oh brother. Teen girl dramatics.*

Erika turned to me, her nose inches from my face. "Your daughter just ripped up her English homework that she spent all evening on!" Had she saved the paper on her computer? No.

"What? Casey!" I was exasperated. Did she have some kind of self-destructive impulse? Despite all of her bluster and pride, the slightest disapproving tone from me hit her like a sledgehammer.

"Dad, don't you know how much I hate myself? You just make me feel worse!" Her words were a cold slap in the face. Her reaction to stress and adversity was always out of proportion to the circumstances. What had we done to induce this kind of self-loathing, or was this just part of growing up?

The self-loathing became more evident as she made her way through middle school and increasingly turned her rage inward, the hyperbole becoming ever more strident.

*"You make me feel like I'm subhuman!"*

I couldn't tell what was normal anymore or what should have sounded the alarm bells. We just wanted Casey to be like the other kids, so we looked for signs of "normalness" and they were there in abundance.

The vast majority of the time, she was still delightful, happy, and charming, a good student who would have made any parent proud. The professionals had to be right. She was just a bit of a drama queen like a lot of teenage girls. So it was easy for me to overlook her more troublesome behavior.

Since taking her out of therapy with Dr. Darnell, we had turned back to our friends, and once again they reassured us that there was no reason to panic. We were good parents and Casey was a good girl. This was fairly normal—though irritating—behavior for a middle schooler. That's what I wanted to hear, and I found that people were eager to tell us what we wanted to hear.

Still, we'd laid down the marker of consequences for bad behavior and had to make good on our threats. Erika was adamant that Casey go back to therapy, and I wasn't about to fracture the parental alliance.

———

We found Casey's next therapist, Tori, at Apple FamilyWorks, a community-based mental health center in San Rafael. She reacted to the prospect of more therapy as if Mom and Dad were about to send her off to a Soviet gulag.

*"I HATE YOU!"* she spat as she yanked her bedroom door closed. I was furious at her—a thirteen-year-old acting like a spoiled, bratty two-year-old totally devoid of coping skills. Why couldn't she grow up and accept that things couldn't always go her way?

When tears wouldn't work, she resorted to relentless negotiation to wear us down. Erika and I were convinced that if Casey didn't become a writer, she'd have a promising career negotiating arms control treaties.

*"If I go to therapy and I don't like it, I get to drop out!"*

*"If I go to therapy, then I don't have to do any chores!"*

*"If I go to therapy, then I demand an increase in my allowance!"*

Perhaps she was angry and humiliated because her parents forced her to see a therapist in a low-rent district of San Rafael rather than the chichi therapists in Larkspur that her friends went to.

After several months, we met privately with Tori to discuss their progress together. Sitting in her office, I spoke frankly. "Casey won't stop complaining about therapy. She refuses to get in the car no matter what we say or do." We were spent.

Tori responded, apologetic. "I understand. At first she started to open up and talk, but then after a while she refused to cooperate."

"Do you run into this problem often, with teenagers who simply refuse to work with you?" I asked.

"Honestly? Very rarely."

Erika spoke up. "Why do you think she's so resistant, Tori, when other kids aren't?"

"Well, she *is* very strong willed." Tori paused to think. "She's just an extremely private person." Once again, we had no discussion of her early abandonment, the orphanage, or her adoption.

We agreed that it was counterproductive to force Casey into therapy as long as she resisted. So, with great reluctance, we stopped the sessions with Tori. Casey would have to understand that this concession was with conditions. She needed to maintain her grades and keep her behavior under control or she'd be back in therapy. But next time—if there was a next time—we'd let her choose the therapist if it would motivate her to go.

# TEN

Casey entered Redwood High School in Larkspur as a fourteen-year-old freshman in the fall of 2004. With about fifteen hundred students, it was four times the size of her middle school, Del Mar, and drew kids from the surrounding towns of Corte Madera, Kentfield, and Greenbrae. The student body was more socioeconomically diverse than at the Tiburon schools, where the kids lived in a bubble of relative privilege.

In a way, Redwood's size afforded the opportunity for a middle schooler to reinvent him- or herself, shake off an unwanted nickname or reputation, and cast a wider net for new friends. It was a fresh start. But it also meant change, and I knew how hard it was for Casey to adjust to the unexpected. She'd had many of the same friends since kindergarten, and while some of her friendships had been strained over the years by breakup, betrayal, or rejection, there was still a measure of comfort in those familiar faces.

Several of her best friends—Roxanne, Maryse, Max—had gone away to private schools. Others—such as Joel, Julian, Ben, and Emily—enrolled at Tamiscal, a small, alternative independent-study school. I hoped Casey wouldn't be intimidated by Redwood's size. She would need to keep up with a heavier workload and start thinking about college. Maybe she'd put her writing gift to good use by contributing to the student newspaper. She might even find a boyfriend.

She'd never had a love interest that I knew of, but then, many of her girlfriends hadn't either. It wasn't that they were antisocial—far from it. They were in constant contact with one another, but it was often through online chats or texts from the privacy of their bedrooms.

Since she'd wormed her way out of therapy with Tori, Casey had been in good spirits. Erika and I were worn down, often disregarding our parenting instincts and house rules by ignoring a rude remark, backing away from a defiant challenge, or capitulating to a demand just for the sake of peace. It was humiliating to feel our authority regularly undermined by a teenager, but we'd do almost anything to ward off a meltdown. Perhaps, we told ourselves, by showing kindness and forbearance, we could coax, rather than force, good behavior from her.

In one such instance, I walked through the front door at the end of the day from work. Casey was sprawled on the sofa, her dirty, sneaker-clad feet propped on our new coffee table next to a can of Diet Dr Pepper missing its coaster. She was engrossed in a video game, The Legend of Zelda.

My instinct was to snarl at her lack of respect; she'd broken two house rules—no shoes on the coffee table *and* use a coaster. But when she saw me walk in, she extended an arm for a hug and a kiss on the cheek, her face glued to the screen. I melted. All was forgotten.

"Honey, could you please take your shoes off the coffee table?" I asked.

"Oh. Sorry, Dad." She kicked off her dirty shoes and planted her bare feet back on the coffee table.

"Thank you."

Of course, our families and friends saw this as a sign of parental weakness, but then, they didn't live in our house. The reward for temperance was well worth the sacrifice of authority Erika and I had over our daughter.

———

Casey seemed to make the transition through freshman year smoothly, but by her sophomore year, the A's and B's that she'd proudly produced since grade school had slipped to C's and D's. Even English—her strong suit—had suffered. She could have counted on an easy A but was down to a D-plus. There was no question that she understood the material; it was about her inability to complete assignments on time.

Letters from Redwood addressed to *Parents or Guardians of Casey J. Brooks* arrived in the mail with increasing regularity, reporting a growing list of tardies, unexcused absences, and missed assignments. This violated the spirit of our cease-fire over therapy, but we were conflicted over how to handle the situation.

Erika felt we should have stuck to our agreement. There should be harsh consequences for this academic slide. She was probably right but I was, again, loath to confront Casey and upset the peace in the house. After all, these were just warnings. It wasn't like Casey had gotten busted for drinking or drugs.

In truth, I was just plain tired of parenting my daughter. She was a constant chess match, a constant challenge. I was worn out from trying to hold a job, keep a roof over our heads, and protect our family from imploding. Confrontation was a last resort.

Casey seemed to have anticipated a conversation over her grades and the letters from Redwood when Erika and I sat with her in a moment of calm in the kitchen one day after school.

"I know what you guys are going to say." She covered her head with her hands in a gesture that could have been rehearsed. "I suck. I'm an idiot. You don't have to remind me."

I bit my lip. "Casey, honey, you know you're none of those things. We just want to know if you need help."

She rolled her eyes. "*No*, Dad. I can handle it!"

"We can get you a tutor," Erika offered.

"Mo-*om*, I don't need a tutor. I just have to hand in a paper for English and that'll raise my grade from a D-plus to a B."

Erika persisted. "Casey, we just want you to know that we can get you help if you want it."

She hopped up from her stool, spun around, and shot off to her room, her arm outstretched and palm turned up to signal STOP as she mouthed, *Thank you!* Our attempt at a family meeting lasted all of three minutes.

But true to her word, Casey completed her paper and raised her English grade to a B. Still, she was perfectly capable of A-level work, and knowing how high she'd set her sights for college, she'd need to buckle down and get the work done for a chance at a top-notch school—if indeed that was what she wanted.

She complained about being bored at Redwood. The courses weren't sufficiently challenging. She shunned extracurricular activities, griped that Redwood kids were too materialistic, shallow, and phony, and lamented that she had no friends there anymore. She pestered us constantly.

"I hate Redwood. Why can't you send me to a private school?"

"Because we moved to Marin for its excellent school system, and if we send you to a private school we'll have no money to send you to college."

"I'll pay my own way to college!"

*Yeah, like you promised to walk Igor and pick up after him. As if.*

She found a boarding school online in Massachusetts that had a unique hybrid curriculum of high school and college. Ever the shrewd negotiator, she tried to convince us of its practicality.

"Dad, if you send me to this school I can get my college degree in, like, three years and you'll save money!"

"Casey, you're fifteen. We're not sending you across the country to a boarding school."

"Why not?"

"Because you're too young and the schools here are perfectly good."

"Da-*ad*. Puh-*leze*?"

In another attempt at compromise, Erika and I agreed to let her apply to Tamiscal—where a number of her friends were—even though we feared that its independent-study program would be a disaster, considering that she couldn't seem to manage her time at Redwood. Besides, Tamiscal had a reputation, whether or not deserved, as a repository for slackers and stoners. But we recognized that Casey needed some control over her life and we left it to her to complete and submit the application. She never followed through.

There was an odd contradiction of sorts between her fragile self-image and the high standards she set for herself and everyone around her. She despised most Redwood teachers, calling them "stupid" or "lame," yet beat herself mercilessly over seemingly minor mistakes in her assignments. She craved respect and recognition for her intelligence but it had to be genuine; she could smell a fake a mile away.

Despite her grumblings over Redwood, there was one teacher who'd won her over—Mr. DiStefano. He was a former Wall Street bond trader who had left his career and marriage behind in his forties to start a new life in California teaching Advanced Placement social studies and economics. His success in the business world impressed her and he became a mentor. He got her in that unique way teenagers need to feel appreciated and respected by an adult other than their parents. She talked about him constantly, agonized over her homework for him, and worried when he was out sick. Mr. DiStefano was probably a pivotal factor in Casey's decision to stay at Redwood.

# ELEVEN

One Saturday morning while Casey was at a sleepover, Erika and I sat outside on the patio with our coffee and newspaper, enjoying an unusually warm December day, dressed in our terry-cloth bathrobes. A hummingbird poked its long beak into a feeder hanging from the side of the house. Erika took a sip of coffee and cut short our moment of peace.

"There's something I need to talk to you about."

"What?"

"One day I was standing outside Casey's bathroom door when she was in there. It sounded like she was throwing up." Erika paused, watching for my reaction. "She was gagging and spitting."

"Yeah, so?"

"I knocked on the door and asked if she was all right. She said she just ate some canned olives on a pizza that made her sick. Then she took a shower."

"So she had a bout of food poisoning." I looked up at the sky, listening to a distant foghorn from the bay near the Golden Gate Bridge.

Erika fixed a disapproving gaze on me. "I've noticed her doing that pretty frequently lately. She may be purging, like she's bulimic."

Erika had begun snooping through Casey's computer, her suspicions aroused by this latest round of disturbing behavior. Whereas my parents respected my privacy as a teen, Erika grew up in a home where parental intrusions into her private life were routine. She'd seen that Casey had visited websites dealing with depression, anorexia, bulimia, and cutting, and suspected that she could have gotten into this as early as middle school.

I pursed my lips. "Ay-ai-ai."

"There's one more thing," she said. "I've noticed Casey wearing these fabric elastic bracelets around her wrists all the time when she isn't wearing a long-sleeved shirt." She waited for me to react. "Whenever I asked her about them or tried to touch them she'd wave me off and wouldn't let me get near them."

"Yeah?"

Erika wrinkled up her mouth as if she'd tasted something sour. "I think she's been cutting too."

I let out a quiet moan. "This child will be the death of me."

Erika took another sip of coffee and pressed me. "I think we need to get her back into therapy."

I was still grappling with Casey's wobbly academic record.

"Do you think this could be a phase?" I asked.

"I don't know."

"What about the cutting? Have you ever seen what's under those wristbands?"

"No."

"Maybe she's not cutting," I said, almost as a question. "You know she doesn't like us fussing with her clothes. Hell, I didn't like my parents touching me either when I was her age."

"Well, I think her behavior is very suspicious." Erika kept her gaze on me, apparently waiting for my reaction.

There was a part of me that didn't want to know what was under those wristbands. If I didn't know what was there then maybe I wouldn't have to deal with it. As everyone said, Casey was just a bit high strung. This was just a phase. It would pass. I wanted to believe that Erika blew everything out of proportion, but I also knew how observant she was, always digging. I remained in denial. Out of fatigue, I just wanted things to go away. It was too much. Why couldn't Casey be like the other kids so that I could focus on my own life?

I gave Erika a pleading look. "Honey, this is a lot to take on all at once. You know how Casey is. It'll be hard enough just confronting her about school." Erika arched her eyebrows, looking apprehensive as I made my case. "Maybe she'll get over this stuff. She'd go ballistic if we were wrong about the purging and cutting."

"O-*kay*." Erika sounded unconvinced.

———

Later that afternoon, Casey blew through the front door. Erika and I were sitting in the living room, where Erika repaired a necklace for a friend while I worked on a crossword puzzle.

"Hel-*looo*!"

She dumped her sleeping bag, pillow, and backpack in a heap by the front door. "Don't worry, I'll pick it up!" She rushed to the bathroom. "I had a good time at Caroline's!" She was wearing her prized ripped jeans, Astro Boy boots, and a black tank top that showed a hint of cleavage. The fabric elastic bracelets were wrapped around her wrists. She was in a good mood.

When she came back into the living room, I took a long

breath and spoke up. "Casey, we need to talk to you for a minute. Could you sit down, please?"

She put her hands up as if to shield herself from our bad vibe as she hurried past us to her room. "I'm not talking to you right now. Not when you use that tone of voice," she said. "Please leave me *alone*. I don't want you to spoil my good *mood*."

My voice remained firm. "Casey, you don't get to choose. This is about sch—" Her door slammed and the lock clicked. *God damn her.* We got up from the sofa and walked to her door. I gave it a knock.

"Ca-*sey*, open the door, *please*." I jiggled the doorknob. Erika's voice rose. "Casey, open this door!" Silence. Erika handed me a screwdriver. I popped the lock open and we stepped in. Casey lay on her bed, her dirty boots on the comforter, glaring at us.

I started in. "We need to talk about your schoolwork. We gave you a chance to turn this around yourself but it isn't working. We're still getting letters from school."

"Dad! Can't you see how hard I'm working! I'm up late every night!"

Erika joined in. "Casey, you're up late on iChat! You got a D in Algebra and your B in English is now down to a C-minus! How're you going to get into college with those kinds of grades?"

"Shut up, Mom! You didn't even finish college!" She tested our limits.

Erika looked as if she would slap her, but I stepped in. "How dare you talk that way to your mother! Look, missed assignments, tardies, absences. That's unacceptable. Remember the deal about therapy?"

Casey started crying. "Okay, I know I suck! Don't you think I already feel like *SHIT*?"

"Please don't curse." I hated her cursing; our attempts to

model appropriate self-expression seemed useless. "Now, what are we going to do about this?"

She curled up in a ball on her bed, burying her face in her hands, weeping. "I was going to tell you if you'd listen to me that I was going to see my teachers after school to work on this. They said that would help get my grades back up."

Her crying usually wore us down, but this time Erika's voice was shrill. "Casey, stop that crying! We know you're faking it!"

Casey sat up on her bed, looking straight at Erika. "SHUT UP, *YOU*! YOU SUCK! YOU MAKE ME CRAZY!"

Erika lost it. "NO, *YOU* SHUT UP! *You're* the one who drives everybody crazy! And by the way, what are those bracelets for!"

*Shit!*

We weren't going to bring this up. Casey screamed at the top of her lungs. "GET OUT!" Erika lunged at her, grabbing the bracelets. "I know you're purging in the bathroom too!"

I stepped in between them but Casey scratched me and tried to bite my arm. I raised my hand impulsively to hit her, catching myself, but it was too late. She looked at me with sheer contempt. "Oh, good one, *Dad*! Now *you're* going to hit me! GET . . . OUT!"

I tried damage control. "Casey, wait . . ."

"GET *OUT*!" She collapsed in a lump on her bed. I pulled Erika away to keep her from getting kicked by Casey's flailing feet and pushed her out the bedroom door.

"LEAVE! I *HATE* YOU!"

I stood in the doorway, my face hot from shame and anger. The moment I backed out of her room, the door slammed shut, rattling on hinges that had loosened from years of abuse. She pounded on it with her fists and feet, dissolving into an hour-long fit.

I retreated to the relative quiet of the kitchen, where I found

Erika ransacking the refrigerator. She had the trash can propped against the refrigerator door as she reached in and hauled out containers of milk and orange juice, packaged cheese and salami, lettuce and apples, all of which she hurled into the trash. This was perfectly good food. I found myself caught between two women having meltdowns.

"She doesn't want to eat? Fine! I'll throw out all her food!"

"Honey! Hey! Stop!" I had to physically restrain her in a bear hug until she settled down.

"God damn her! I hate her!" she cried.

"No you don't. You hate her behavior."

"Little bitch. Look what she made me do," she mumbled, wiping away tears as she reached into the trash to retrieve the food. I guided her to the counter stools, where we sat down, exhausted and defeated, praying that the neighbors hadn't heard the commotion.

———

Fortunately, Casey's meltdowns wore her out. She'd be calm the next day after exorcizing whatever demons lurked inside and tormented her. Still, I was afraid she'd hold this incident against me forever, another excuse to hate my guts.

This wasn't the father I wanted to be, despised by my own child. I just wanted to be a normal dad with a normal child, whatever "normal" was. I loved her but didn't know if she loved me.

Later that night, I wrote her a note in a move toward détente. *Dear Casey. Sorry I lost my temper. You know how much I love you. Love, Dad.*

I affixed my smiley face at the end, went to her room, and tried the door, but it was locked. So I slipped the note underneath.

By eleven o'clock I was lying in bed, watching the local news. Erika was asleep but I wanted to stay awake for *Saturday Night Live*. Jack Black was hosting and Neil Young was the musical guest. Our bedroom was dark except for the flitting TV. Out of the corner of my eye, I saw a figure standing in the doorway, silent like a ghost. It was Casey.

"Hi, honey." I was happy to see her. Maybe she wanted to talk.

She'd composed herself. "You know, you never just talk to me," she said. "You have no idea who I am."

My heart sank. I was desperate to reach her. What did she mean, I had no idea who she was? *Casey, who are you? Tell me. What am I doing wrong?*

"Honey, you won't let me in. You know how much we love you." Maybe that was a crack in her armor, a chance to connect. "Casey, please sit down for a sec." But she was like a frightened deer wary of human contact and turned away. My words didn't come fast enough.

She was gone.

What if I'd found the right words, calmed her down and coaxed her into talking with me? Perhaps she would have peeled back her suit of armor and revealed a bit more, shared with me who she really was, fighting, crying, and screaming on the other side of that battered door, the one that I was never allowed to open, someone just a foot away.

She could have told me that I was foolish to try to love her, an abandoned piece of human wreckage. Was that what she wanted to say? Was she terrified to tell me for fear that she'd be abandoned again? But there was no amount of hate she could spew at me to drive me away. I'd never let that happen. Even when she used the weapon "You're not my real parents," my response was "Tough. You're stuck with us and we're not going anywhere."

If only I could have convinced her that Erika and I loved her unconditionally. Our fights were just reactions to her outbursts, not her. We just needed her to help us help her.

# TWELVE

Casey and I passed through Sacramento on I-80 heading north toward Lake Tahoe. It was February 2006—Presidents' Day weekend—and we'd planned to go skiing for a few days in Squaw Valley over her winter break.

Vacations together had become increasingly rare, as Casey, a soon-to-be sixteen-year-old, preferred the company of her friends. She hated being seen with us in public, sometimes going to extremes to avoid being spotted by her friends. She'd slump down in the car or insist we walk ten paces behind her at the mall, as if she were in a witness-protection program.

We took advantage of this trip to Tahoe to be together while we still had a chance. Unfortunately, just before leaving, Erika came down with the flu, and it looked as though the trip would be off. But to my amazement, Casey insisted that she still wanted to go alone with me. I was flattered but also worried that we'd run out of things to talk about. Erika had no such problem and could always be counted on to fill awkward dead air with conversation.

On the road I felt comfortable with long stretches of Zen-like, meditative silence. Casey sat in the passenger seat next to me wearing one of her favorite outfits—a tomato-colored, quilt-patterned hoodie, her ripped jeans, and a rose-colored T-shirt with the label FCUK from the French Connection U.K. store in New York. She loved the edgy wordplay and the connection to New York, where she hoped to live someday. Her beat-up Converse All Stars lay in a heap on the floor, my prerequisite for allowing her to use the dashboard as a footrest while she listened to her iPod.

Since our last major blowup, Erika and I had done nothing to follow up on our threat of therapy over Casey's schoolwork. There had been no discussion of Erika's suspicion about cutting and purging. Sometimes our fights with Casey were like boxing matches where we retreated, bloodied, to our corners after a particularly bruising round.

It was easy to be lulled back into complacency on the good days and put off the uncomfortable responsibilities of parenting. Our failure to take action and our tendency to postpone threats of consequence hung over me like a dank cloak.

In the heat of her profanity-laced rages, I sometimes forgot that there was so much good between us, the "normalness" that we craved. When she was three, Casey danced around our living room in Simsbury insisting that she'd marry me and we'd name our child Casey. At seven—when being together with Dad was a treat rather than a burden—Erika dolled her up in a little black dress, purple stockings, party shoes, and a dab of lipstick and mascara so that we could go to the Father-Daughter dance together. At thirteen, we went on an early-morning walking marathon through lower Manhattan searching for a coveted pocketbook she'd found on the Internet. That same year, she blew my mind by giving me an expensive watch for Christmas (with a little help from Mom), and I began to understand her attitude toward gift giving. If you were going to give, give big, otherwise don't bother.

I will never part with that watch.

"Hey, Dad." Casey unplugged one of her earbuds and shook out her hair. "How long till we get there?"

"Umm, probably an hour or two, depending on traffic."

She groaned and looked out the window. "Man, this place is pretty cutty, Dad," she said, referring to the procession of malls and subdivisions that lined the freeway north of Sacramento.

"Yep." I smiled at her Marin County teen vernacular.

We continued north into the Sierra foothills, past Auburn, Colfax, Yuba Gap. By Kingvale we saw snow on either side of the freeway. I took a risk.

"Sooo . . . are there any boys at school you're interested in?" She shot me a look of disgust, her mouth ajar, as if she were about to vomit. "Dad, I can't believe you asked me that! I have more important things in my life right now!"

It was hard for me to believe that boys weren't tripping over themselves for her, but I was biased. I had a pretty good idea which boys she thought were cute, like Nathaniel, Dylan, her friend Emily's brother David, even our minister's son Steven. She spent a lot of time with her friends Julian and Max, but they seemed platonic. In fact, all of her relationships with boys seemed platonic.

Perhaps sensing my thoughts, Casey said, "You know, I'm not *gay*, Dad, if that's what you're thinking." I glanced at her, a bit surprised by her statement. "And by the way, don't think I'm going to get married and have kids, because I'm not. I hate kids."

I stifled a laugh. "I just want you to be happy, sweetie. You know that."

We were silent again, drifting back into our thoughts. I was pretty sure she hadn't been sexual with anyone. But that wasn't unusual. Most of her girlfriends hung out in a pack. We suspected that some of them were sexually active, some not. Casey seemed to put intimacy of any sort at arm's length. I didn't care whether she was straight or gay. I just didn't want her to live her life alone and I feared that her tendency to push people away could leave her stranded.

At Donner Summit the snow was well over the roof of the car. It felt like we were driving through a freezing white corridor of fifteen-foot-high snow walls. We stopped at Truckee for a snack and a quick bathroom break, then made the last leg of the trip to Tahoe City.

I had whiffed on the boyfriend thing, but while I had her captive I took another risk. "Honey, have you ever thought about your birth mother?"

I was hit with another look of revulsion. "Dad, why would you even ask me that?" she muttered while shaking her head.

"I don't know. I was just wondering if you'd ever want to talk about it."

"With *you*?" She cranked up her iPod until I could hear the rap beats exploding from her earbuds. It was one of my few, timid exploratory missions into her biological past—a reality check. And of course my inquiry was met with her usual slap-down.

It was nearly four o'clock when we checked into our room at the Travelodge, a budget chain in Tahoe City—two queen beds, desk, table and chairs, cheap prints on the wall, cable TV, coffeemaker with bad coffee, bathroom. Nothing fancy, but clean, comfortable, and functional. It looked perfect to me. Casey practically choked as she gave me her verdict. "*Ahg!* This place is *janky*." She threw her bag on the bed closest to the bathroom. "Dad, why do we have to share a room?"

"We're here to ski, not to hang out in our room all day. Besides, a room in Squaw Village costs over twice as much as this place."

"Caroline and Ian's dad has a condo at Squaw."

"Well, first, they're up here all season long, and second, they obviously have a rich and generous dad," I said with a drip of sarcasm.

"Da-*ad*. Stop it." She hated it when I made the slightest negative remark about her friends, even in jest.

—

It had actually been a good day. I loved being with Casey when she was happy, and looked forward to a day of skiing as I drifted off to sleep while she watched *Project Runway*.

The next morning, we joined the procession of mud-splattered traffic inching its way from Tahoe City to Squaw Valley; it took a half hour to drive the five miles and park, but I still had plenty of time to get Casey to her snowboarding lesson. We took the gondola to High Camp and found the meeting spot for the snowboarders. Casey noticed some other boys her age and shooed me away. I was to pretend not to know her until instructed otherwise. We were to meet an hour later when the lesson was over.

I made my way over to the Siberian Express quad lift and joined a group of three, listening as they talked to one another about the weather and trail conditions. Looking down at the skiers and snowboarders gliding silently forty feet below us, I fantasized about Casey and me racing down the slopes, Casey swaying back and forth on her snowboard with me in hot pursuit. It would be so gratifying to see her enjoy something she felt she'd mastered, and it would do wonders for her self-esteem.

At the appointed time, we met in front of the High Camp outdoor restaurant. She sat outside in the snow with one boot buckled into the snowboard, looking disheartened. I slid up next to her.

"Hey. How was it?" She poked at the snow and shrugged. Maybe she was just tired.

"Do you want to ski a bit? I'd love to see what you learned." She remained silent.

"You wanna go inside and get something?"

"Yeah, whatever." She pulled herself up and unbuckled her boot.

We got hot chocolate inside and sat by the window. I tried to get her to talk but she was unresponsive. It seemed the snowboarding lesson didn't go as she'd hoped, and I knew better than to press her into a conversation. She wanted to be left alone. But now we had a problem. How would we make the two-thousand-foot descent from the mountain?

I tried again, gently. "Honey, if you're tired, we don't have to stay."

She stared at her hot chocolate. "What about you? You want to ski."

She was right. It was a gorgeous day and I hated to waste the opportunity, not to mention the money I'd spent. If I had some fun while she waited for me, perhaps she'd learn a valuable lesson that the world didn't revolve around her. But I couldn't enjoy myself knowing that she was miserable. I gave in.

"I don't care. I can go. Maybe we should take the gondola down."

She looked at me, rolling her eyes. "That's lame, Dad." Taking the gondola would've meant losing face. She was too proud for that. She was determined to get down on her own steam. Maybe she'd get a second wind that'd boost her spirits. It was impossible to coax a smile out of her.

We finished our hot chocolate, went back outside, and buckled ourselves into our gear. Normally, the three-mile trip to the base of the mountain would've taken about twenty minutes, most of it a gentle descent, but there were a couple of steep, tricky areas.

We pushed off from the restaurant, and I let Casey go ahead of me. She wobbled slowly for about ten feet before falling backward and sitting down in the snow. As I pulled up beside her she shot me an accusatory look of resentment, as if this was entirely my fault.

I extended my hand. "Want some help?" She ignored me, pulled herself up, found her balance, and coasted slowly for another twenty-five feet before stopping at a flat straightaway. I stopped next to her. "Wow, honey, that was great!"

We made it to the base after an agonizingly slow hour and a half, punctuated by crying and cursing fits. Several times Casey threatened to abandon the board and spend the night on the mountain before I coaxed her back on.

By the time we made it to the bottom, her nose was runny from crying and her hair was caked with clumps of wet snow. She was exhausted and angry with herself. If only she'd had more patience. I wanted to wrap my arms around her, kiss her wet hair, and cheer her up, but I knew she'd just berate me.

"C'mon, honey. Let's pack up and go home." It was pointless to stay.

She looked down at the snow, mumbling, "I'm sorry I ruined everything," slurping back tears and snot on her sleeve.

I felt my heart in my throat. "Sweetie, don't be silly. I just wish you had a better time on the snowboard." I went to put my arm around her but she pushed it away.

I'd gotten used to rejection and tried not to take it personally anymore. I just hoped she knew that I'd never reject her no matter how difficult she was.

We drove home in silence. Casey never went skiing or snowboarding again. It was another reminder of her inability to tolerate failure, like the time she crashed and burned on the Yerba Buena skating rink when she was eight. If she couldn't do something perfectly, it wasn't worth doing, and that robbed her of so many opportunities.

# THIRTEEN

Casey finished her sophomore year with a GPA equivalent to a low B, respectable for most kids but not up to her personal standards, and she probably gave herself a good thrashing. It was less about us and more about her disappointment in herself.

We found ourselves, once again, in a cycle of defeat. Casey refused our offers of help or tutoring, and we felt powerless to console her when she was down. With summer break coming up, we hoped she'd forget about school for a while and go back in the fall refreshed.

She played soccer and lacrosse during the summer break, but it was more social than athletics. For exercise, she'd drag out her Dance Dance Revolution video game and mimic the TV moves on her dance pad in the living room as if it were a Jane Fonda workout tape.

We were shocked when Casey expressed an interest in a work camp program in Alaska sponsored by our church youth group, a pleasant surprise coming from someone who insisted that she was an avowed atheist. Since she had few extracurricular activities, the trip could have been a wonderful growth experience for her and would spruce up her résumé for college. The program attracted a broad cross-section of kids, from self-proclaimed atheists like Casey to the very devout. When she came home, she complained about proselytizing "Jesus freaks" who wouldn't leave her alone. When pressed, though, she admitted that she enjoyed the housepainting and a boat trip to see a glacier up close, so it wasn't a complete waste.

Erika continued to keep an eye out for evidence of Casey purging. Since we'd first raised this concern with her, there were fewer strange noises from her bathroom that would have suggested she was throwing up her food. Either it had been a phase or she'd simply gone underground, out of earshot. But she still had some questionable eating habits, and it had become increasingly difficult to get her to eat with us. When she did, she'd pick at a salad and ignore the protein before racing back to her room to tackle her homework, or so she said.

She complained regularly of stomach problems, but a trip to the doctor revealed nothing—no poisoning, appendicitis, or ulcers. Her diet seemed to consist mostly of cereal, ramen noodles, sliced bread, salad, and, of course, Diet Dr Pepper by the case. She claimed to be a vegetarian.

Erika was more attuned to Casey's eating habits than I was because home-cooked meals had been an essential part of her family life growing up. But nagging Casey did nothing but provoke a fight and a door slammed in the face.

She didn't seem much different from her friends or the other kids in the neighborhood. They were vegans, vegetarians, and raw foodies who stayed up too late glued to the Internet, watched too much TV, and slept too late. Some couldn't eat wheat, others gluten or dairy.

Casey stopped wearing the fabric bracelets around her wrists, and there was no evidence of any more cut marks. She'd confided to Erika that some of the girls were just curious about cutting. It was an experiment and it was over. Nothing to freak out about.

—

Casey started her junior year at Redwood in the fall of 2006. Erika and I hoped for a turnaround from the year before, but she continued to struggle with the precarious attendance and performance record that we first saw in sophomore year. There was no consistency to her grades. They were at one extreme or the other.

| A.P. European History—A | Enjoy having student in class |
| Pre-Calculus—F | IN DANGER OF FAILING |

This was especially worrisome because she had less than two years to raise her GPA for college admissions. She couldn't afford many more attendance problems or incompletes, particularly because she had her sights set on some pretty competitive schools—NYU, Bard, Reed, Bennington. I was petrified that failure to gain admittance would send her off the deep end.

But there was something else brewing that was even more troubling.

—

Erika raised the subject one Saturday on a walk with our friend Sharon and her dog, Joy. It was Indian summer, shorts and T-shirt weather. Sharon had on a pair of big black sunglasses. We walked along McKegney Green in Tiburon, making our way to a small white gazebo by the water. A local family who'd lost their seven-year-old daughter to a mysterious disease forty years earlier had donated it to the town. It was a very tranquil spot. We sat down.

"This is such a cool little place," Sharon said, admiring the latticework.

Erika sighed. "Yeah. It's just so sad because it was built for a little girl who died."

We were silent. Igor and Joy walked up to us from the bay water, panting, their tails wagging, sticking their noses up to say hello. Then they wandered back to the water. Erika broke the silence. "I need to share something that's bothering me."

*Uh-oh.*

"I was putting some clothes away in Casey's room and I found an empty bottle of Skyy vodka in the back of her drawer."

My mood sank. Sharon, normally the consummate cheer-leader—Ms. Positive—had a look of concern on her face as Erika continued. "I was also looking through her pocketbook and I found a pack of cigarettes and a glass pipe."

I was taken aback. "What do you mean? Like a crack pipe or hash pipe?"

"A hash pipe," Erika answered.

"Oh." I was curiously relieved. At least she wasn't smoking crack. "Why were you going through her stuff?"

Erika was annoyed. "What do you mean, why was I going through her stuff? Aren't you concerned that your daughter might be doing drugs?"

I resented Erika's accusatory tone but I knew she was right. Of course I was concerned. It was just so overwhelming. First the grades, then the purging and cutting, now this. Upon Erika's insistence, we had formed a parents' group to connect with

Casey's friends' parents so that we could all keep tabs on their outings, parties, and overnights. We thought we had the substance issue covered.

I drank and smoked pot when I was her age, but I hid it and my parents never caught me. Now that I was a parent, I was faced with the ultimate irony. I still had a weakness for a chardonnay and a toke, and I thought I had to hide it from my daughter, who, apparently, was also toking.

Why did Erika have to be so goddamn observant? Couldn't we just look the other way like my parents did when I was a kid?

I grasped for a way to respond. "Do you have any idea how often she's been getting high?"

"Nope."

Sharon weighed in. "A lot of kids are into drugs and alcohol at Redwood, but I'd be especially concerned about Casey. You don't know much about her physiology and what she might have inherited. Some kids get through this and others become addicts." We watched a seagull glide in to land on the rocks by the water. Igor was on full alert; he sprang but the gull flew away.

I thought to myself that maybe this wasn't as bad as it sounded. Perhaps Casey was a casual drinker or toker—like at parties—but didn't buy it for herself. I'd never seen her wasted, and I had doubts that she did bong hits first thing in the morning before school like some kids I'd suspected or even knew about in my own youth. And her grades? They weren't stellar but she wasn't flunking either. Still, we had a serious problem with our daughter and couldn't sit back and do nothing.

She'd had more than enough chances, and we'd bent our own rules too many times. I let out a long breath. "I guess we have no choice. We've let her slide hoping she'll turn around, but now we have to make good on our promise to send her back to therapy."

Erika, sensing my anxiety over another confrontation, turned to Sharon. "After the last two therapists, Casey's been dead set against going back. Have you ever heard of a child who refuses therapy?"

"No. I can't say that I have."

I remembered something that Erika and I had discussed after we ended Casey's sessions with Tori. "Why don't we let her pick the therapist—within reason, of course."

Sharon perked up. "That's a great idea."

The thought of another therapist disaster left me numb. Dr. Darnell was essentially useless. Tori was an improvement but still failed to connect with Casey. The church work camp trip to Alaska only reinforced her vow of atheism. What if we shipped her off to a grandparent? My mother would have loved to pamper her, but perhaps my mother-in-law's Polish discipline would have been the better remedy. We were running out of options.

We stood up and took in the inscription on the bronze plaque in the middle of the gazebo.

CHILD OF SUNLIGHT, CHILD OF STARLIGHT,
CHILD OF MOONLIGHT, GRACE,
SHINE YOUR JOYOUS LIGHT OF LOVE ON ALL
WHO FIND THIS PLACE.

I shook my head. "I can't imagine losing a child."

"I don't even want to think about it," Erika said. We called Igor and Joy back from bird patrol and walked back home.

———

The only way for us to have this conversation without Casey running out the door was to wait until she was in her room and stand in the doorway to block her only exit. That moment came soon enough on Sunday, the day after our walk. The door to her room was open, so Erika and I poked our heads in.

It looked like Hurricane Katrina had swept through—clothes, books, shoes, pillows, CDs, empty cans of Red Bull and Diet Dr Pepper were strewn everywhere. Her papasan chair in the corner was barely visible under a pile of dirty laundry. Her new IKEA platform bed was fairly neat, the white comforter tucked in, stuffed animals arranged around the edges. The pink squeaky doll that we'd given her in Poland poked its head out from a pile of pillows. And of course there was her ever-present comfort pillow, now threadbare from years of wear and restuffings.

Casey and I had painted her room a dark royal blue. The darkness was both mysterious and calming, complementing the carpeting in the room, a powder blue except for the big yellow stain in the center, compliments of Igor. For all the chaos on the floor, Casey didn't like clutter on her walls. There was a large, black-framed poster with the words from *Romeo & Juliet* in the corner; a white-and-orange poster over her bed from the movie *Trainspotting*, about junkies in Scotland; and a small white metal road sign from a pedestrian underpass in Paris. It read: *Entrée Interdite aux Vélos et Motos.*

She was in her usual spot, hunched over her computer, sitting on her ratty secretarial chair.

She'd given herself a makeover by changing her hair color from dirty blond to a medium soft brown. Instead of parting her hair and clipping it to the side, she let it fall to her shoulders and cut her bangs into a shag like Cleopatra—she looked stunning. Her ripped jeans had given way to skinny straight jeans, but she still had on her white hoodie—she was always cold.

I took a breath, realizing in the moment how nervous I was.

She was the one who should've been nervous. "Hey there," I called out tentatively. "What're you doing?"

She took a swig of Red Bull. "Talking to Julian. We're gonna hang out later."

We were about to spoil her evening plans. She wasn't going anywhere. I felt a pinch in my stomach as we stepped into her room; Erika pulled out the empty blue bottle of Skyy vodka. "Casey, I found this in the back of your drawer the other day. How did it get there?"

Casey glanced at the bottle, nonchalant. "I don't know." She shrugged. "Somebody must've left it there." She had no fear. I, on the other hand, imagined myself in a panic confronted like that by my parents.

Erika stood firm. "I find that hard to believe, Casey. I think you put it there."

"Well, it's *true* . . . *MOTHER*!" she spat. "And I don't appreciate you questioning my *integrity*!"

I stepped in between them. "Casey, calm down."

She shot me a look of contempt. "No, *you* calm down!"

Her eyes teared up and her shoulders quaked from a stifled whimper. Crocodile tears. I was losing patience and spoke firmly. "Casey, you need to stop crying and acting like a two-year-old every time we have a serious conversation."

Her whimpering turned into bitter sobs.

Erika picked up the exchange. "There's something else, Casey. I found a pack of cigarettes and a pipe in your pocketbook." She pulled out the evidence and showed it to Casey, who looked at it wide-eyed, not with fear but with rage.

"WHAT? YOU WENT THROUGH MY POCKET-BOOK? HOW *DARE* YOU!"

I was weak-kneed but Erika didn't flinch from a fight. "You

can forget about going anywhere tonight, young lady. You're grounded and you're going back to therapy!"

"WHAT!" We backed out of the room. Casey kicked the door shut, locked it, and hammered at it with her fists and feet.

"You're ruining my *LIFE*!"

We left food out for her but she stayed in her room for the rest of the night.

———

Our offer to let Casey pick her next therapist softened the blow somewhat. Not surprisingly, she chose a Larkspur therapist after a rave review from one of her girlfriends who was a patient. There were as many shrinks crammed in between the Lark Theater, the Left Bank Brasserie, and the Silver Peso Bar in this charming little ritzy town as there were on an Upper East Side block of Manhattan.

For the right price, you could see a Reiki practitioner, an acupuncturist, an astrologer, a hypnotherapist, a psychic, a marriage and family counselor, a life coach, and, of course, a resplendent buffet of psychiatrists. No problem was too bizarre in Marin County. You could just as easily find someone to potty-train your puppy as to break your fifteen-year-old of his or her addiction to Oxycontin.

The new therapist's name was Dianne. Casey's first appointment was Columbus Day, 2006. I had the day off and drove her. We were quiet in the car, as usual, as we pulled into the parking lot behind Dianne's office. I offered her a sympathetic smile, but she ignored me, grabbed her pocketbook, and left the car, marching up the stairs to Dianne's office.

Erika and I had already met with Dianne. Her specialty was teenagers. She reminded us of Mama Cass—full-figured, long blond hair parted in the middle, gold satin kimono and lots of jewelry. She was an earth mother type who insisted on enveloping us in bear hugs. Her office was cozy and comfortable, with three oversize black leather chairs perfect for napping. Erika and I had a good feeling about her after an hour together. I prayed that this time we'd found a confidante for Casey. Maybe Dianne could connect with her where others had not.

An hour after dropping her off, I was back in the parking lot waiting for her. Within minutes, Casey bounded down the stairs and hopped into the car. Much like the aftermath of her first meeting with Tori, she seemed calm and genial.

I tried to catch her eye. "Well, dare I ask how it went?"

"Fine." She dug through her pocketbook for something. "Hey, Dad. I can't find my Starbucks gift card, *a-and* I want to get a Café Americano?"

"So you want me to take you there?" I loved the lilt in her voice when she was in a good mood.

"Uh, yeah? And, can I borrow some money?"

"Don't worry. I'd be delighted to buy you one." We drove to Starbucks like two people comfortable in each other's company.

———

Over the next few months, Casey continued weekly therapy sessions with Dianne and didn't resist the reminders when Erika or I had to take her there. It was hard to know how the process was going. Sometimes when we picked her up, she was chatty and relaxed, other times sullen and uncommunicative. When asked about Dianne we'd usually get a grunt, a shrug, or a one-word answer, like "Fine." And because of doctor-patient confidentiality, Dianne was limited in what she could disclose about their sessions.

We were reluctant to press Casey for more information. We

couldn't afford for her to walk away from a third therapist. As long as she continued to go without a fuss, we were happy.

The dreaded letters from Redwood stopped showing up. Either Casey's work habits had improved or she'd become more adept at intercepting the letters at the mailbox. She agreed to a tutor for her precalculus and he seemed to help. She was able to raise her grade from an F to a D, hopefully on the way to a C, at least.

She seemed to have realized that she was running out of time to polish herself for college applications if she didn't want to end up at community college.

———

Casey's eating habits continued to be problematic. Most of the time she ate separately from Erika and me, claiming that school-work beckoned. We could see how hard she worked and didn't want to discourage her newfound discipline, so we reluctantly excused her from the table.

Her unorthodox diet consisted mostly of starches and Diet Dr Pepper, but she never lost an opportunity to show us when she was eating salads or fruit.

We suspected that she was probably sneaking the occasional drink or joint, but had no proof. When Erika rifled through her pocketbook—much to my discomfort—the only contraband she could find was the stray empty pack of Camel Lights.

As much as we hated her smoking cigarettes—and, probably, pot—we decided not to confront her. Let it go. She had a nice group of friends—artists and musicians. I just prayed it was nothing more exotic than pot. Considering all the weed my friends and I smoked when we were their age, and I still did, I couldn't hold that against her without seeming hypocritical.

We enjoyed some stretches of calm again in the house. I no

longer felt a pit in my stomach when I walked through the door from work for fear of stepping onto a land mine. Perhaps this meant the sessions with Dianne were working.

So far, all signs were relatively good and we lavished Casey with praise. Perhaps feeling a boost in self-confidence, she pushed me for an increase in her twenty-five-dollar weekly allowance, deploying her powers of persuasion and negotiation for maximum effect.

*"I really should be getting more money for going to therapy and getting my grades up."*

*"I get the stingiest allowance of anyone I know. Everyone else gets at least fifty dollars a week."*

*"If you raise my allowance, I promise to do chores around the house."*

Unfortunately, her rationale for a raise rested largely on the notion that she should have been rewarded for doing things she was expected to do anyway. We were pretty generous in doling out other money, but she had to come to us to ask for something specific on which we could render an opinion.

I was unmoved and reluctant to give in because I suspected that any financial gain would go toward cigarettes, alcohol, or weed. If I couldn't stop her from using those substances, at least I could delay the inevitable. This was one debate I actually won, because I had control over the money.

# FOURTEEN

During her junior-year Christmas break, Casey got a job as a seasonal helper at the Williams-Sonoma store in her favorite mall, the upscale Village at Corte Madera. She did everything from greeting customers to working the cash register and wrapping gifts in the stockroom. Dressed in a forest-green Williams-Sonoma apron, with a white name tag that said CASEY, she was a big hit with the staff and clientele. She put her beautiful smile, charm, and cute dimples to good use, earning eleven dollars an hour, which quickly swelled her wallet.

Even though she'd turned sixteen in May, we still had to shuttle her back and forth to work because she hadn't bothered to get her driver's license, something we were in no hurry to enable. The short drive gave us a chance to hear her stories about boring staff meetings, bitchy bosses, and a sales contest where the prize was a two-hundred-dollar stainless-steel saucepan.

She befriended a boy named Clive from Tamalpais High, and told us how he made her crack up when they worked together in the stockroom. One afternoon at the end of her shift, she practically skipped toward me as I waited in the car, a huge smile on her face. As she hopped in, out of breath, she spoke excitedly.

"Ohmygod, Dad! Guess what? You'll never believe what just happened!" Her words tumbled out of her mouth. "I just waited on *Phil Lesh* at the store!" Phil Lesh is a legendary rock star, the bassist for the Grateful Dead, one of her favorite bands. She looked like she was about to faint from her close encounter with stardom. "He was so cool! I mean, he was *so . . . normal!* He bought a blender!"

"Wow, honey, that's exciting!" I loved the Dead too.

She noticed me admiring her. "Dad, could you stop looking at me and go?" She hated being stared at, even if it was in adoration. As I pulled away, she fished through her pocketbook, pulled out her red Razr cell phone, and flipped it open.

*"I'vegottatextJulian!"*

I loved her to pieces at that moment.

———

Soon after New Year's Day, 2007, Casey was back in school. Her bank account was stuffed with more than eight hundred dollars, which she'd made from her job over Christmas break, the equivalent of eight months of her allowance. Work had given her self-esteem a much-needed boost. She'd dismiss compliments from Mom and Dad, but it was entirely different when praise came from bosses and customers, especially famous customers.

I began to feel as if the years of fighting, worrying, and false starts were finally behind us. Casey was in the hands of a good therapist, she was intensely focused on schoolwork and college plans, and it seemed she felt good about herself. If she could just keep it up until we got her off to college.

But she couldn't.

⸻

I walked through the front door from work on a Friday before the Martin Luther King, Jr., Day weekend to the sound of Erika's screams reverberating through the entire house. "Casey Brooks, you are impossible!"

Part of me wanted to turn around and leave.

"John? Is that you?" Erika marched into the kitchen. I grabbed a bottle of chardonnay from the fridge to fortify myself for the clash that was sure to come. Erika looked like she'd blown a gasket. She was practically out of breath, her eyes wet with rage.

"You need to talk to your daughter!" She pointed toward Casey's room. "Do you know what she said?"

"How could I know what she said? I just walked in." I poured myself a glass of wine and took a long gulp. Maybe vodka would've been better.

Erika scowled. "You better take this seriously! She says she's not going back to therapy!"

"Shit." My head drooped. "Did she explain why?"

"Why don't *you* ask her?" Erika took the half-full wineglass from my hand and finished it, while I poured myself another glass and took a gulp, feeling a calming buzz.

I tried to stay composed. "Could you stay here while I talk to her?"

"Sure. I'm done talking to her."

Casey's bedroom door was open. Looking at it, I was disgusted. The lock was broken from our numerous attempts to jimmy it open with a screwdriver. The cracks running through two of the inset panels where she kicked it were the result of her on-again, off-again raging fits. That had been a new door. Didn't she have any respect for the things we worked for? I pushed it open and stepped inside.

It was quiet, the lights were off, and the window shades pulled down. The dark blue color of the room made it look like a cave except for a narrow shaft of light through the skylight. Casey was in bed burrowed under the covers, her back turned toward me. A lock of her brown hair poked through a gap where her cream-colored down comforter exposed her head. Her comfort pillow was a mangled ball by her head, an appendage of her body. She couldn't possibly be sleeping—just pretending, a ploy to get me to go away. She certainly wasn't afraid of me; she just wanted to avoid a conversation. I sat down on her ratty secretarial chair in front of her desk.

"Casey?"

She pulled the comforter over the remainder of her head that wasn't covered. As angry as I was, I still found her adorably child-like.

"Casey, I need to talk to you."

A muffled voice answered from under the covers. "I know. You hate me."

"I don't hate you, honey, but please let me at least see your face."

"No."

"Casey, Mom said you refuse to go back to therapy. Why?"

She turned around on her back, lifted the comforter off her face, and stared at the ceiling, away from me. "Dad, it's a waste of your money."

"I think I'll decide that."

"Besides, she's just stupid."

"You mean Dianne?"

"Dad, my friends know ten times more than she does, and I can talk to them."

I sat back in the chair to think.

"You can't make me go back, you know."

"Excuse me, Casey. I'm the parent. I think that's my decision, not yours."

*Damn her! How do I control this kid?* I couldn't force her to do anything and she shrugged off any threats of punishment. Did she have any respect for me at all or was I just some useless buffoon, easily manipulated to fulfill her needs and make her happy? Did I even exist as anything other than a conduit for her to get what she wanted? What did I mean to her? Did she love me or just use me?

She had to love me, as much as she was capable of loving anyone.

I think.

Still, I couldn't help but feel like a failure, utterly incompetent as a parent.

"Casey, I'm extremely disappointed with you. Do you know how hard Mom and I have worked to get you help? We'll talk to Dianne about this."

She pulled the covers back over her head. I was too tired to fight.

———

A few days later, Erika and I were back in Dianne's office, slumped in the oversize black leather chairs. She watched us with a sad expression, sympathetic to our latest setback as Erika and I sat holding hands. In her forty years of practice, Casey was one of only two teen patients who'd quit therapy. How would she explain this?

I asked her. "Dianne, you're the third therapist we've been to. No one has been able to get her to open up. You're the professional. What are we doing wrong?"

Dianne thought for a moment. "I can't go into detail because of patient confidentiality, but I don't think it's you."

"Okay, so what is it?"

"Well, I've thought quite a bit about her early childhood—the abandonment, the orphanage. Have you ever heard of something called *attachment disorder*?"

"No." Why did everyone have to have a disorder? ADD, ADHD, OCD. Now attachment disorder.

Dianne continued. "Children with attachment disorder have often been abused or abandoned at a young age. Many of them are orphans who've missed out on the nurturing of a parent. They often have difficulties bonding."

"Dianne, how is that possible?" I said. "The orphanage was so many years ago. How could that have an effect on her today? She's had a perfectly normal life, and most of the time she's a great kid."

"The first twelve months of a child's life can be crucial to her development," Dianne said. "The effects of Casey's childhood could be deeply buried in the subconscious."

We sat, mute, until Dianne moved on to another topic. "But there's something else about Casey that *really* troubles me."

Erika and I leaned forward, waiting intently.

"It's her drug use."

Dianne went on to paint a disturbing picture of teen drug use in Marin County, a virtual epidemic, exacerbated by the availability of more powerful and addictive strains of marijuana, hallucinogens, cocaine, and prescription drugs. She had seen the devastating effects over the years on dozens of teens firsthand—mood swings, limited impulse control, inability to concentrate, social withdrawal, poor judgment.

Erika shot me a scowl. "I knew it."

Dianne continued. "All of the symptoms are there—the

rages, tantrums, academic problems, antisocial behavior. It's that crowd she hangs around with. They're a bad influence."

I chewed on my lip as I listened, bristling at the accusation that my daughter had a drug problem and that her friends were somehow enabling her destructive behavior, like pushers. I glanced at Erika, perched on the edge of her seat.

"Do you think we should put her in rehab?" Erika asked.

"At this point I don't have enough information to say one way or the other, but I wouldn't rule anything out."

I laced and unlaced my fingers as we sat in silence again. We'd failed at parenting and failed at therapy. And now we were told that the root cause of Casey's problems was either a lack of bonding or drugs or both.

Was she a hopeless case or was there a magic pill that could fix her? Medication had always been my last resort.

"Dianne, what do you think about medication?" I asked.

"Well, I can't make a diagnosis," she replied. "But it might be wise for you to have a psychiatrist evaluate her. My associate, Dr. Palmer, is an excellent child psychiatrist and can prescribe medication. He's right across the hall."

Perhaps sensing my frustration, Dianne said, "Look, I know this is a lot to digest. I haven't spent much time with Casey, so I can't be certain of anything yet. There's a lot we don't know about early childhood trauma. And without any information on her physiology or family history, Casey's drug use could have serious consequences."

I sank back into my chair and stared at a Japanese watercolor on the wall. The fighting at home, anxiety over schoolwork, the purging, cutting, drugs, and fruitless meetings with therapists had been debilitating. We couldn't keep changing therapists.

I looked to Dianne for help. "Where do we go from here?"

"I'd love to continue seeing Casey," she said. "But she has to want to come back, and right now she doesn't."

I cradled my face in my hands while Erika rubbed my back.

Dianne looked heartbroken. "I'm so sorry. She really is a wonderful girl. I was drawn to her instantly."

We got up to leave and Dianne gave each of us a long hug. As we turned to leave, Dianne spoke up. "You know, there's a good book about attachment disorder you might want to check out." Erika jotted down the title and author.

On our way out to the car, I tried to grasp the magnitude of Dianne's words. Attachment disorder? Drugs? This was serious stuff that was hard to take in. Every pediatrician and therapist who'd seen Casey since she was a toddler had been amazed at how far she'd come. No one had ever mentioned any connection between her behavior and her infancy in the orphanage.

I resisted Dianne's implication that Casey was some kind of druggie, but she was the expert. I wasn't qualified to challenge her opinion. Though I'd come around to considering medication, it still worried me after stories I'd read about their potentially deadly side effects.

We were running out of options. Erika and I agreed to set up an appointment for Casey to see Dr. Palmer.

———

At home, we found Casey sitting on the sofa in the living room, watching TV and eating a bowl of Cracklin' Oat Bran. Igor was curled up on his pad on the floor next to her. Knowing that we'd just come from Dianne's office, she said in her most charming voice, "Don't worry, I finished all my homework." She shoveled a spoonful of cereal into her mouth. "Oh, and I got a B-plus on my science test. Sorry, I couldn't wait for dinner. I was hungry."

She didn't appear the least bit anxious about our meeting with Dianne, and I felt like she was playing me again with her charm. But the sight of her together with her loyal canine friend was oddly hypnotic and took the edge off the tension that had hung over us since we'd walked through the front door.

"So what happened?" Casey asked.

I rummaged through the refrigerator looking for nothing while Erika checked the phone for messages, both of us ignoring her. *Give her the silent treatment and let her squirm for a while.* It was about the only weapon we had left.

"Hel-*looo*?" she said.

Erika and I walked into the living room and sat down on a love seat facing her with grim looks on our faces. "We all agreed that you should be in therapy." She scowled at me. "But we also agreed that you have to want it and obviously you don't right now." Her face relaxed. I could almost hear her inner voice screaming a triumphant *Yes!* with a hearty, imaginary fist pump.

"And one more thing." I didn't want to bring up Dianne's lecture about drugs just yet. It would just lead to another fight, and I had no fight in me at that moment.

"We've made an appointment for you to see a specialist to be evaluated for medication." I purposely substituted the word *specialist* for *psychiatrist* so that Casey wouldn't freak out about another probing therapist. I expected another burst of protests, but Casey remained silent, staring sullenly at the TV.

I tried to catch her eye. *"Okay?"*

She shrugged and stared straight ahead.

Erika picked up. "Before you go out and celebrate, Casey, you need to know that none of us—Dianne, Dad, or I—are the least bit happy about this. So since we can't force you to go to therapy, we expect your behavior to be nothing less than exemplary or you're grounded—forever."

I cringed at the thought of Casey permanently grounded. That meant that we'd all be grounded, but I remained quiet as Erika continued. "That means no nastiness, no cursing, no more letters from school about your attendance and work, none of this purging, and most of all, *no drinking, smoking, or drugs*."

Casey gave Erika an icy glare. "I don't *purge* and I'm not into *substances, MOM!*"

I stepped in, speaking to her calmly but firmly. "Casey, knock it off. I suggest you not abuse our trust, because I'll tell you right now, if we find anything on you, we may have no choice but to send you away for treatment."

———

Later that night after dinner, Erika and I retired to our bedroom, drained from the events of the day. Erika was in the bathroom brushing her teeth as I picked up the *Chronicle*. Flipping through the Bay Area section, I stopped at the obituaries.

An announcement and photograph caught my eye. A sixteen-year-old Mill Valley boy had "died suddenly" but they didn't say how. I recognized his name. It was the boy Casey worked with at Williams-Sonoma just a month ago. Erika walked out of the bathroom in her white terry-cloth bathrobe, towel-drying her hair. I couldn't believe what I was reading. "Honey, you're not going to believe this."

"What?"

"Remember that boy from Mill Valley Casey liked so much who worked with her at Williams-Sonoma?"

"Yeah?"

"He died."

With her hand to her mouth, Erika practically whispered. "Oh my God."

I learned the next day through a Google search what "died suddenly" meant. The boy who made Casey laugh at work had jumped off the Golden Gate Bridge.

# FIFTEEN

Every time we pulled Casey out of therapy, we'd been rewarded with some family harmony. In the months that followed our separation from Dianne, Casey was a model teenager. When a fight brewed, we managed to keep it down to a minor skirmish. Erika and I considered this a victory. It seemed we'd allowed Casey to teach us how to parent her by avoiding conflict altogether.

We took her to see Dr. Palmer. She didn't resist the idea of medication. Despite my misgivings, perhaps a magic pill *would* be an effective substitute for invasive therapy sessions. Several of her friends swore by antidepressants such as Zoloft and Prozac.

I was comforted to hear that Dr. Palmer treated teenagers first with natural remedies that minimized the risk of side effects, before resorting to more powerful prescription drugs. He put Casey on a B vitamin supplement called Inositol that had been shown to reverse major health issues such as depression, anxiety disorder, hyperactivity, and obsessive-compulsive disorder. Though she'd never been diagnosed with any of these conditions, this seemed promising. We were at the end of our rope, grasping at anything. Other than Dianne's brief reference to an attachment disorder, no one drew a connection between her behavior and her past.

Unfortunately, Inositol was not the magic pill. Casey complained of irritability and insomnia. With her patience short, she gave up, so we dragged her back to Dr. Palmer.

He put her on Lamictal, a mood stabilizer, claiming that it helped "calm the mind." "People feel like themselves again," he said, "without any negative side effects." Perhaps that was the perfect antidote for Casey's symptoms. But after a week, she complained of headaches. She was tired of therapists, psychiatrists, and medication and wanted to stop everything. No amount of cajoling, pleading, or threats would sway her.

Erika and I were back in our same old place—exasperated, exhausted, and furious with our daughter for refusing to cooperate with our repeated attempts to help her. Unwilling to continue throwing money at our problem, we decided to give in and take a break from Dr. Palmer. Summer was approaching; maybe we'd revisit this again in the fall.

Maybe there was something to this attachment disorder that Dianne had mentioned. Erika found the book at the library that Dianne had recommended. It was called *Social Intelligence*, by Daniel Goleman. But as we read through it, we found that it had little to do with adoption or attachment at all. It was mostly about the biology, brain science, and behaviors associated with human interaction and relationships. Neither Erika nor I could understand what Dianne was thinking.

With that, the issue of attachment disorder was laid to rest.

At the end of her junior year in June 2007, after she'd turned seventeen, Casey passed her driving test and got her license. With her access to wheels, we had another carrot to dangle in front of her for good behavior. We also had something new to worry about—Casey getting maimed or killed in a car accident.

With school over, the weekend party circuit was in full swing. One Saturday evening, Erika and I sat together on the sofa in the living room with a bottle of wine, getting ready to watch a DVD that we'd been curious about. It was a bit gruesome, and we didn't want Casey to see it.

It was a documentary called *The Bridge*, about people who'd committed suicide from the Golden Gate Bridge. It was controversial because for the first time since the bridge had been built in 1937, it exposed its dirty little secret as the world's top suicide magnet. We were aware that people jumped from the bridge, but couldn't fathom why anyone would do such a thing. I couldn't shake the thought of the sixteen-year-old boy who jumped, the one that Casey liked so much from Williams-Sonoma. I wondered if she knew.

We settled into the sofa and I pushed PLAY. As the opening credits rolled in front of an image of a fog-shrouded bridge, Casey walked into the room, fully equipped for an evening out. She was wearing her favorite tomato-colored quilted hoodie over a long black sweater with gray stonewashed jeans and suede boots, her teal Marc Jacobs handbag slung over her shoulder. She glanced at the TV as I fumbled for the remote.

She looked perplexed. "What're you guys watching?"

"Nothing," Erika said. "Just a documentary."

She glared at us as if she'd just caught us smoking pot. "Are you guys watching that bridge movie?"

I tried to change the subject. "Casey, we'd just like to watch our movie. Okay?"

She hated to be kept in the dark. Looking at us suspiciously, she shook her head. "God, you guys are so sick, watching people kill themselves." There was a moment of awkward silence. "So . . . can I have the car keys?"

Even though she was a relatively new driver, she whined that she was the only kid at Redwood without a car. But Erika and I considered wheels a privilege, not a Marin County entitlement.

We had designated my VW, with more than 100,000 miles on it, as the "shared car." Thus far, Casey had gained our trust by taking it out and getting herself and the car back in one piece. She would have to live under that restriction, a small price for transportation.

As we followed her to the front door, I fished my keys from my pocket. Turning to her, dangling the keys in my hand, I made her work a bit for them.

"Homework done?"

"Yup."

"Room picked up?"

"Yes, Dad." I bent down to kiss her cheek and caught the fresh scent of Marc Jacobs's Eau de Parfum. No cigarette smoke, thank God. With a playful grin, she snatched my keys and was stepping out the door when Erika piped up. "Casey, wait a minute!" She turned around, her jaw hanging open, a look of annoyance on her face.

"Do you have a flashlight?"

"Yes, Mom."

"And the Mace?"

"Ye-*es*. In case you forgot, I'm not five years old anymore."

"Make sure to bring water so you don't get dehydrated and check the gas so you don't run out!"

Casey inched her way toward the car. "Mom, I'm not a retard."

"Okay, drive safely!" Erika waved excitedly as I stood next to her with my palm raised in a perfunctory salute.

Casey snapped back. "No, Mom, I'm going to drive into a tre-*ee*. I'm not an idiot!"

She gave us a sheepish smile and wave from the driver's seat as she buckled in, adjusted the mirror, and lurched away from the curb. I felt a mixture of pride and anxiety as she drove away.

———

The main focus over the summer of 2007 was college. Casey would be sending out applications in the fall, so we used the summer break to narrow down choices and visit campuses. Her A list was a collection of small, competitive liberal arts schools: Reed, Bard, Bennington, Marlboro, and Hampshire. Other than Reed, these were all East Coast schools. Casey wanted an East Coast experience, having long since forgotten about her early years in Simsbury. More important, however, was her desperation to get as far away from Mom and Dad as possible, something that she reminded us of constantly.

*"When I go away to school, don't expect me to call every day like Mom does with Grandma."*

*"I'm not going to visit you over the summer. I'll probably have an internship in New York."*

*"And by the way, what am I gonna do for transportation? I'll need Dad's car."*

Having gotten used to her mouthing off, I didn't take it personally. I wasn't about to pick a fight over every insult that spewed from her mouth. Besides, I didn't think she really meant it.

One Sunday afternoon in June, I found her at the kitchen island flipping through a slick glossy brochure from Reed College that had just come in the mail. Reed was her top pick at that moment. I put my hand on her shoulder and kissed the top of her head. "Hello. What's this?"

"It's a brochure from Reed College." *Itsabrochurefrom Reed-College.*

I looked over her shoulder. "Hmm. Good school."

She sighed. "Yeah. I probably won't get in, though."

I winced. "Don't say that, honey. You know how smart you are." I put an arm around her shoulder and she let me give her a squeeze.

"Dad, my grades suck and I blew the SAT."

"Your grades last semester were fine, honey."

"Yeah but my GPA sucks. I got like a two-point-eight."

She needed to hear a compliment from someone other than me to let it in. "Well, the SAT isn't everything and you still have this coming fall semester in senior year to get your GPA up."

"Dad, you don't get it. The average GPA for Reed is like a three-point-nine. My friend Alex has like a four-point-two."

I looked at her, puzzled. "I thought the most you could get was a four. How did Alex get more than that?"

She casually flipped to another page. "A.P. courses. Alex is Asian and he's hella smart." I chuckled at Casey's reference to the overworked, overachieving stereotypical Marin kid. But I was also shocked at the admissions standards for schools that were a notch below the Ivy League.

We looked at photographs of a bucolic college campus—cherry blossoms in front of a red-brick building, a kid working on his laptop in the library, a teacher pointing at a cluster of formulas on a blackboard.

I wondered how many hours Casey had spent in her room in front of her laptop poring through images of a college life she'd be part of in another year. She envied her friend Roxanne, who went to boarding school in New Hampshire. I bet Casey imagined it like Harry Potter's Hogwarts and wanted a place like that for herself.

"So what do you like most about Reed?" I asked

"The senior thesis program." *Theseniorthesisprogram.*

"What's that?"

"It's this hella huge project you do in senior year. You give an oral presentation, then they bind your thesis and put it in the library."

I was taken aback. "You *like* that?"

"Yeah!" she said, excited.

"Sounds intimidating to me, but then I know you're a smart cookie." I admired her genuine hunger for knowledge. She was nothing like I was in college, wasting my time following the path of least resistance to get my ticket punched.

She patted my shoulder. "Those were the good old days, huh, Dad?"

We looked at a page devoted to Reed's campus dogs. There was a picture of a long-nosed greyhound. "Ohh*hh* . . ." she whined. "I wish I could bring Igor."

"Then you have to feed him and pick up his poo." She playfully punched my shoulder.

"Dad, do you have any money to send me to college?"

"Why would you even say that?"

She shrugged, looking down. "I thought we were broke."

What was she fishing for? An excuse to be disappointed? "Okay, Casey. First, we're not broke. Second, your college is already paid for. Third, that's not your concern anyway." She snorted a faint sign of approval and I added, "Luckily, I just have one kid."

She gave me a mock scowl.

"Fortunately, the schools you picked don't focus on just one thing," I said. "You need to show them what a gifted writer you are and get some good recommendations."

"Mr. DiStefano said he'd give me a good recommendation."

I smiled. "See? C'mon, honey, try not to worry. You've got plenty of time. You're gonna be fine." I hoped I sounded convincing. I dreaded the thought of a meltdown—or worse—if she didn't get into one of her dream schools.

"Yeah, right." She sighed and flipped another glossy page of the brochure.

——

Later that night, I was alone in the living room on the sofa watching *60 Minutes*. One of Apple's cool commercials came on for the iPhone that was due to come out in late June. Casey shuffled through the room on her way to the kitchen from her bedroom. She was wearing her black hoodie, skintight jeans, and fuzzy lamb's wool slippers. Stopping at the TV, her head dropped, mouth wide open. She pointed at the screen and croaked. "I want one!" Unfortunately, her birthday had passed and she already had a cell phone.

"Everybody wants one," I said.

"Ohh*hh* . . ." She looked at me with pleading eyes.

"Besides, you just got that Razr phone."

She put on her best pouty five-year-old act. "I know-*ow* . . ."

"Maybe someone will be nice and get you one for Christmas."

"Da-*ad*," she whined. "That's like six months away-*ay*." She was playing with me again, and probably didn't expect me to drop four hundred dollars on a new phone. We tried to teach her the virtue of delayed gratification, waiting for special occasions to dole out those kinds of gifts.

Feigning disappointment, she dragged herself to the kitchen, grabbed a Diet Dr Pepper from the fridge, and headed back to her room, glancing at me as she walked by, her lower lip stuck out in a pout. At seventeen, she still knew how to tug on my heart. I turned back to the TV. Mike Wallace was interviewing Jack Kevorkian—Dr. Death.

Minutes later, Erika walked in from the bedroom and planted herself between the TV and me, a grave look on her face. Had I done something wrong, like throwing out the newspaper or pouring out her cold coffee before she was done with it? I sat up. "What's the matter?" The look on her face worried me.

"I want to show you something." She stood rigid as if trying to contain an explosion. I followed her to our bedroom. She closed the door and pointed to my dresser. "Look at what I found in our daughter's room."

My dresser looked like the scene of a drug bust—a formidable collection of pharmaceuticals and paraphernalia that Erika had arranged in a neat display. In stark juxtaposition to this pharmacy sat two framed photographs—one of the three of us at Casey's baptism in Simsbury and one of her smiling from her new bike when she was six.

I gazed at the evidence. There was a glass pipe that I picked up and sniffed—grass. A small, clear, self-sealing bag contained what appeared to be a few grams of pot. But what caught my eye were things I didn't recognize. I picked up a gray plastic film container—the same kind I used as a teen to store my grass—popped the lid off, and poured the contents into my hand. It was something organic, brownish with no smell. Mushrooms? An orange plastic pill bottle that had once contained my Paxil prescription was now half full of round white pills with smiley faces printed on them. What the hell were they? Acid? Ecstasy? Another clear plastic bag contained yet more pills that had a strange organic look to them. Erika stood next to me, arms crossed, close to tears.

I was so stunned I couldn't respond. I'd been duped by my teenage daughter and now felt like a world-class chump. Like a gullible idiot, I'd prayed this whole problem would blow over or fix itself. Maybe we *did* need to carry through on our threat to send her away.

Screw college.

"Goddamn her," I muttered, disgusted with myself and my daughter.

Erika picked up the bottle with the white pills. "We've lost control over our daughter." Looking at the pipe, pills, and weed on my dresser, it seemed as though there were more drugs than a single person would need for casual use.

Maybe she had a serious addiction, but how was that possible when we saw her every day? If she was doing drugs under our noses, she must have had a talent for never looking high. She always looked perfectly straight. Could she have been dealing? I wanted to put her in front of a firing squad. "Let me get her in here," I grumbled.

Erika stayed in the bedroom while I went to Casey's room. The door was open, so I walked in. She was in her usual place, hunched over her desk with her iPod plugged into her ears. She looked up at me innocently and pulled out an earbud.

"Casey, could you come with me, please?" She followed me to our bedroom, where Erika waited by my dresser. Casey looked at the arrangement of substances and paraphernalia as if they were totally alien to her. Erika stood silently while I asked, "What is this?"

Casey shrugged. "I have no idea."

Erika couldn't contain herself. "Casey, I found all this in your room!"

Casey's face flashed red. "WHAT?! YOU'RE NOT SUP-POSED TO SEARCH MY ROOM! THAT'S A VIOLATION OF MY *PRIVACY*! HOW *DARE* YOU!"

She looked at both of us, indignant. She was angry at *us*? Man, this kid had chutzpah. I picked up the pill bottle and shook it in front of her face. "What the hell is this, Casey? Ecstasy? Acid? Where did you get this stuff?"

She shook her head at me, her eyes filling with fear. "This isn't mine, Dad! Someone wanted me to hold it for them!"

Erika jumped in. "Oh, really? Who?" That was exactly what I wanted to know.

Casey's fear turned to rage. "I would never rat out my friends to *YOU*!"

Erika fired back, "Casey, are you dealing this stuff?"

She shot Erika a piercing look. Pushing past me, she marched back to her room. I called after her, "Casey, get back here!" Her door slammed and she proceeded to pummel it, her screams echoing through the house.

Erika and I planted ourselves on either side of her door like two hostage negotiators. Trying in vain to control my temper, I told Erika under my breath, "I want to strangle this kid."

"I HEARD THAT!" Casey screamed from the other side of the door as she gave it another hard kick.

I wanted to take a sledgehammer to that door.

"SOON I'M GOING TO BE EIGHTEEN AND I'M

GOING TO GO AWAY!" she howled. "YOU WON'T BE ABLE TO BOSS ME AROUND. I'LL NEVER CALL YOU AND YOU'LL JUST GET OLD AND *DIE!*"

Now *I* hated my own daughter. Her behavior wasn't normal—the vicious tirades, primal screaming, smashing her door. It was like a force had taken over that she couldn't control.

I tried pushing on the door with my shoulder. Though virtually inoperative from our many attempts to pop it open, we had decided to take the lock off in a futile attempt to treat her privacy as a privilege, but Casey had a grip like a vice on the other side. *Jesus Christ, she's strong.* Meanwhile, she wouldn't stop screaming, crying, and kicking. *God damn it, the neighbors will surely call Child Protective Services this time.*

Erika and I took turns trying to twist the doorknob. We were scared to death of what might happen on the other side of that door. I was tempted to kick it in, what was left of it.

After a half hour of trying unsuccessfully to pry open the door and get her to calm down, I'd had enough. I talked to her through the door as if negotiating with a terrorist. "Casey, if you don't stop, I'm calling the cops!"

Another kick. We left for the kitchen, where I dialed the Tiburon Police.

I walked back to Casey's door. It was open, but now the bathroom door next to it was locked. We hadn't noticed that she'd slipped out of her room and into the bathroom while we were in the kitchen.

Erika hurried to the bathroom door. "CASEY, WHAT'RE YOU DOING IN THERE? OPEN THIS DOOR!" She pounded on it, but there was no sound from the other side. She screamed, "CaSEY!"

An image flashed through my head of my worst nightmare—

breaking down the door to find Casey on the floor inside, unconscious, covered in blood, a razor blade in her cold, limp hand. Even though we hadn't seen any evidence of cutting in a long time, we still tried to hide the blades in the house.

The doorbell rang. Erika joined me as I opened the door to a Tiburon police officer. His cruiser was parked on the street. He was young with a strong build, military-style haircut, and wraparound sunglasses. His name tag read GILBREATH. He could've been Casey's older brother.

We explained the events of the past hour, leaving out the part about the drugs, though I was tempted to teach her a lesson by handing her and the drugs over to law enforcement. Officer Gilbreath was calm and professional as he listened to us.

He asked us to wait in the kitchen while he went to talk to Casey. There was a "click" from the bathroom and I caught a glimpse of a shadow dashing to Casey's bedroom. Thank God she was alive.

After about ten minutes, Officer Gilbreath rejoined us in the kitchen. He didn't say what they'd talked about, but assured us that Casey had calmed down and that she'd be okay.

I apologized profusely as I escorted him to the front door, but he laughed it off good-naturedly. This was probably not the first time he'd had to deal with domestic disturbances in tony Tiburon.

I watched as Officer Gilbreath pulled away from our house, checking up and down the street for nosy neighbors. Looking at my watch, it was 9:40; it felt like much later. We needed to cool down.

Erika and I left Casey alone that night on the condition that she wasn't to leave the house. There was no sense in trying to tackle the drug issue that night. We were exhausted and would deal with it later.

# SIXTEEN

The next morning, as I was getting ready for work, I decided to check in on Casey. Often, the morning after a major blowup, she'd appear refreshed and chipper, acting as if nothing had ever happened. On my way to the kitchen for a cup of coffee, I glanced toward her room. The door was cracked open, so I ventured over and peeked in.

She was gone.

Her bed was made, the mountain of pillows was neatly arranged, and her room was spotless. In fact, it looked as though it had been decluttered down to the bare essentials.

On the hutch above her desk where she kept schoolbooks and tchotchkes she'd collected over the years there were personal things missing: the wax dragon statuette we got her one Christmas, the Buddha she bought in the Haight, the ceramic rhino she asked for on a visit to the San Diego Wild Animal Park, and a small framed photograph of Igor as a puppy.

Her bookcase had also been swept clean. Photo albums I'd made for her, soccer trophies, the Robin Hood American Girl doll, school yearbooks—were all gone. Initially, it didn't strike me as a bad thing for her to organize her room, especially since it was usually a mess. We'd given up hassling her about it; let her live with it.

I turned to her closet, assuming she'd stowed everything away and out of sight. But when I peered in, it looked like it always did—a chaotic mishmash of clothes, some dangling off hangers, others fallen to the floor.

Where had she put all her stuff and, more important, where the hell was she? We had told her not to leave the house. I looked out her window and saw the Saab parked outside. She couldn't have run away, but then, I was never sure what she was truly capable of.

I went to the kitchen and found the *Chronicle* folded on the counter as if it had been waiting for me. An empty coffee cup had been set on top of it. My heartbeat quickened and I thought about calling the police again, but a slip of paper with Casey's handwriting under the coffee cup caught my eye.

*Sorry. I went to Bell Market to get a bagel. Be right back.*

I exhaled slowly. Thank God she was okay. But what was she doing up so early? It was summer vacation and there was no school. There was no time to investigate. The coffeemaker had been set the night before, so I poured myself a cup, taking a few sips, hoping to clear my head as I reached for the *Chronicle*. A sheet of typing paper lay underneath, folded in half. I opened it—a formal-looking typewritten letter from Casey. I was running late but took a minute to scan it.

*Mom & Dad:*
*    I knew this was the only non-confrontational way to get*
*my point across because I doubt in any other situation I would*

134

*be adequately heard. We would engage in some immature and unnecessary arguments, which would solve nothing.*

That sounded mature and reasonable. At least we were having a conversation, albeit by letter; better than no conversation at all. Maybe that was how we should communicate—in writing.

*I'm not saying that experimenting with drugs is part of growing up, but it can be a learning experience. I'm not saying it's right. What I'm trying to say is that experimentation (not addiction) as a teenager can have a relatively positive outcome.*

Great. Spoken like a true devotée of the sixties psychedelic icon, Dr. Timothy Leary, who told us to *Turn on, tune in, and drop out.*

*I am not (this has to be clear) in any way a constant and recreational "drug user." This letter is not a valiant attempt to have you agree to let me take drugs, but I do believe that a mutual agreement (or tolerance) should be obtained between child and parent.*

Boy, this kid had balls. She was asking us to adopt a "Don't Ask, Don't Tell" policy. I would never have dreamed of writing anything like this to my parents. I imagined her as a future William Kunstler, the controversial civil rights lawyer who defended the Weathermen and then went on to defend clients such as terrorists, drug dealers, and arms merchants.

*I know that you both are highly against any sort of drug use. But a one-time discovery of Ecstasy possession is not an indicator that the child (me) is "on the road to addiction." I do not smoke cigarettes, and have smoked marijuana rarely. I am in no way a "druggie." I'm sorry it had to happen this way.*

I disagreed with the entire premise of her letter—that her drug use was negotiable—but was impressed by the way she built her case.

I left the letter on the counter for Erika to read, and went to knock out the coffee grounds in the trash under the sink. The trash was full, so I took it out the kitchen door to deposit in the garbage can outside. When I lifted the lid I was shocked at what I saw: the wax dragon, the Buddha, the ceramic rhino, the photo of Igor, the photo albums, trophies, American Girl dolls, school yearbooks, video games, jewelry Erika had made for her. It looked like Casey had taken her entire life and thrown it in the garbage.

I'd read stories on the Internet that people bent on killing themselves sometimes gave away their possessions. Was she trying to rattle us, or did she just not think this through? Sometimes, in a fit of rage, she could be destructively impulsive.

Once, after a fight, Casey got into Erika's computer and deleted all of her e-mail addresses, just to spite her. Another time, she went to Erika's closet and pulled all of her clothes down from their hangers, leaving them in a heap on the floor. We could never get her to explain her extreme behavior. For all of Casey's bluster, I could never imagine her going to the extreme of taking her life. I could see her running away from home, even taking my car as the getaway vehicle. She was probably trying to piss off her parents, and she did.

Maybe Casey was right. We had no idea who she was.

———

That night, Erika and I sat locked in our bedroom; she sat on the bed while I perched across from her on a love seat.

We struggled to understand the room-purging incident. Erika's eyes were moist from anger. She told me that she'd spent the morning picking through the trash can to recover Casey's possessions, careful to clean off the coffee grounds, banana peels, and chicken bones. She was almost tempted to leave everything where it was and let Casey suffer the consequences of her impulsiveness. But she couldn't let go of keepsakes that meant a lot to her, even if they meant nothing to Casey.

"Did she explain why she threw her stuff out?" I asked.

Erika dabbed her eyes with a Kleenex and shook her head. "She refused to talk to me. She's just been holed up in her room."

I chewed on my lip in frustration as she continued. "She really worries me, John. The tantrums, the resistance to therapy or discipline, the erratic grades, the drinking and drugs, that call to the police, and now this. I don't know whether she's self-destructive, suicidal, or crazy."

I avoided Erika's gaze, staring at the floor, struggling to respond, but my mind was a blank.

"You know what we should do?"

I looked up.

"We should send her away to one of the schools for kids with behavioral problems."

I grimaced. "Do you have any idea how much those places cost?" She never thought about money.

"Is that all you think about? Money? Why don't you think about your daughter?"

I resented the accusation. Someone had to be responsible for our finances. "If we send her away—*if* we can get her to go—then there goes her college fund."

Erika jabbed at me with her finger. "*If* we can get her to go? We can't let her push us around like this! You're always giving into her and undermining me, so now she doesn't respect me! Meanwhile, she has you wrapped around her little finger. When are you going to act like a father and be tough with her?"

I knotted my fingers as I looked down at the floor.

How many years had we spent trying to "control" Casey's behavior? Why couldn't Erika see that just "being tougher" never worked? Casey was impervious to discipline. I was afraid that outsourcing our parenting to a reform school would further push her away and poison an already toxic environment at home. There seemed to be no alternative that didn't smack of a cop-out, such as grounding. It rarely worked, and besides, she couldn't spend her whole teenage life grounded, could she?

The room-cleansing incident remained a mystery. Despite the harshness of Casey's actions, I thought that Erika still read too much into it. Casey was just being her usual impulsive self. Act first, think later. We hadn't even dealt with the issue of the discovery of the drug cache and the call to the police the night before. That was a whole other issue that had become overshadowed by this most recent crisis. Was she a drug dealer on top of everything else?

Erika's voice was flat. "So if we're not going to send her away—which is what we agreed to do—what do we do now?"

I fell back into the love seat and sucked in a breath of air, letting it out slowly. "I don't know. I'm just worn out. I guess she'll remain banished to her room until further notice."

"You *guess?*"

I shot Erika a glare, tired of her constant accusations since Casey was in grade school that I wasn't tough enough. I had no idea of how strict or forgiving to be with Casey anymore. Her grounding meant that we'd have to keep an eye on her at all times. So we'd all be angry, miserable, and grounded together.

Fortunately, our misery was short-lived. We'd planned a trip back east in July and August to look at colleges. Casey's grounding was lifted after just a few weeks. There wasn't much we could do while we were traveling but make empty threats to deal with bad behavior later. In all likelihood, it would be forgotten or ignored until we got home. After all, a parental threat of punishment was only enforceable at the moment of the offending behavior. It wasn't deferrable.

Casey was excited about the trip. She'd spent hours online dissecting every one of her dream college websites, comparing notes with her other friends, trading intelligence. She was enticed by images of white-steepled churches on college campuses bursting with fall color, and stories of boarding school during her late-night iChat sessions with her friend Roxanne. She had long since forgotten about her early years in just such a picture postcard New England village: Simsbury, Connecticut.

We spent the trip in a fragile truce, driving through New York, Vermont, and Massachusetts in a rented Toyota Camry, visiting five schools in two days. We fought over directions, campus tour schedules, radio stations, restaurants, and hotels. After two days confined like three caged ferrets, we limped into the Hertz drop-off at JFK. Soon enough, Casey would have her freedom and independence and, hopefully, she wouldn't forget us.

# SEVENTEEN

Senior year at Redwood started in September 2007. Erika remained unhappy with my lack of a follow-up response to Casey's drug bust earlier in the summer. She had always resented my tendency to default to a family cease-fire to preserve the peace over confrontation. But time had passed, and in the eyes of a teenager, the statute of limitations—measured in days, not weeks or months—had long since expired. Meanwhile, Casey had thrown herself into her schoolwork and I didn't want anything to distract her.

She worried about the effects of the missed and late assignments and spotty attendance on her once-stellar academic record and, potentially, her college plans. She was determined to raise her GPA to something that began with a three so that she had a shot against stiff competition, and she had only one more semester before she'd send out college applications.

The only way for her to accomplish that in one semester was to sign up for Advanced Placement courses for extra points. She signed up for three, insisting she could handle—even welcome—

the challenge. From past history, I knew that was when she was at her best.

By October, she'd made up her mind about college. Her announcement was a declaration rather than a request for permission—so typical. It was a glorious Indian summer Sunday afternoon under a cloudless sky as Erika and I sat outside. Those were the days we lived for. Casey burst through the screen door in a typically dramatic entrance, plopping herself down in a chair between us, a look of satisfaction on her face.

"Okay, parents," she announced with the flair of a carnival barker. It didn't take much for her to get our attention, especially when she was in good spirits. "I've figured out my college plan." She paused, waiting for us to respond. That was her way of seeking our approval.

I raised an eyebrow. "Really? Please, tell us!"

She slapped the arms of the patio chair with both hands for maximum effect. "I'm applying for Early Decision to Bennington!"

A wise decision, I thought. Bennington was an excellent, though pricey, school with an alternative, artsy bent. It was close to my mother and grandmother in Connecticut. My grandmother was 106 and in shaky health, but we'd been saying that for years and she kept defying the odds. I looked over at Erika, who seemed more guarded, probably unhappy that Casey would leave the West Coast.

"Wow!" I said. "Why Bennington?"

"Because they have a cool work-study program, I met people online who like it there, and I think I can get in through Early Admission," she said, confidently. She'd heard that colleges were more flexible with Early Decision applicants, provided they committed to attend if they were accepted.

Erika was concerned. "What about the schools on the West Coast, Casey?"

She glared at her mother. "Mom, I want to get as far away from here as possible!"

"Casey, that's a very mean thing to say." Erika couldn't hide her hurt.

I tried to gently take Erika's side. "Casey, do you have any idea how cold it gets in Vermont in the winter?" Her idea of winter was probably forty degrees and sunny, like in Tahoe.

"Yeah! That would be so cool!"

Erika wouldn't let go. "Casey, I'm just worried about what would happen if you get sick."

Casey jumped up from her chair. "Mom, that's stupid! Colleges have infirmaries, you know!" She stomped back into the house.

Erika looked at me, exasperated. "Why don't you ever back me up? I'm really worried about her being so far away from home. Other parents decide where their kids go to school. Why can't we?"

I grimaced, as if we could get her to do anything. We just had to let Casey be Casey. Once she'd set a goal for herself, nothing could get in her way, and nobody was allowed to help. She'd racked up an impressive stack of A's and B's in her A.P. courses, and obsessed over her admissions essays, where she would truly shine. If she wanted to shoot for Bennington, I voted to give her a chance to feel good about herself rather than hold her back.

In light of Casey's newfound determination to take charge of the next phase of her life, we decided not to hassle her about the behavioral issues that had plagued us for so long unless they were truly egregious—say, finding a pound of weed stashed under her bed or noticing a dramatic weight loss.

We just wanted to get her off to college. I started to relax. We would get through this.

———

One weekday in October, I had plopped down in front of the TV to watch the local news with a glass of wine. Casey came in.

"Dad?"

"Yeah?"

"Could I talk to you for a minute?" That was odd. She wanted something, probably money.

"Sure." I waited for her to sit down.

"No, I mean in there." She pointed toward my office, something she'd never done before—requesting a private meeting alone with me. I followed her into the office.

She shut the door and we sat down. She had a mischievous look in her eyes. "So, Dad. I was looking for a Motrin the other day and I was in your bathroom." She paused and I looked at her intently. "I looked in your toiletry kit . . ."

When I heard *toiletry kit* I knew what she'd found—*my* stash of weed. My mind raced so fast that I didn't even hear the end of her sentence.

I pretended to stay calm and emotionless, but we both knew where this was going—my nightmare scenario, busted by my own child. On top of being a shitty father, now I was the ultimate hypocrite. Nice going, *Dad*; a Mexican standoff.

As the blood drained from my face, I wanted to melt away and disappear, grabbing for something to say. "Okay, Casey. So what is it you want to say?"

She was loving every minute of this. "I just think what I found in there was very interesting, since you've been so antidrug with me."

I searched for a rational defense. "Casey, this doesn't change how I feel about you and drugs. You're seventeen and we don't know how this will affect your physiology. Mom and I are trying to keep you safe until you're on your own."

"Dad, I'm not a druggie. I know what I'm doing. If you knew me, you'd realize that."

*Ouch.* "Casey, we never said you were a druggie. But whatever I do, I can't condone your drug use. I'd be an irresponsible parent if I did." She was trying to blackmail me.

"We need to compromise."

"No, we don't."

"Dad, this isn't fair."

*Damn her.* I just wanted this to be over and pretend nothing ever happened. "Then what exactly did you have in mind?"

"I want you guys to stop searching my room."

I pursed my lips and rocked back in my chair. Erika would hate me for not discussing this with her and for kowtowing to our seventeen-year-old yet again, and she'd probably continue to search Casey's room anyway. After a moment to think, I looked at Casey wearily. "Fine." She smiled, satisfied, as we got up to leave.

That was the best day of Casey's life.

# EIGHTEEN

Her online application for Bennington was off in plenty of time for the October deadline. Then we waited. A decision was expected in mid-December, sixty days away.

As I watched the other kids going through multiple applications for a springtime response, I understood Casey's decision to apply early. She wanted to spare herself the torture of waiting until spring to learn her fate. She knew herself too well.

The air in the house was thick with silent tension. She'd never had so much at stake before and so much to lose if she didn't get her desired result. I had nightmare visions of Casey receiving a rejection letter.

Despite her insistence that she'd prepared for any outcome, I imagined her falling into a downward spiral, locked in her room crying for days, refusing to eat. Or she could put on a good game face, keeping the disheartening news bottled up inside where it would eat her alive.

By early December, Casey practically stalked our mail carrier, anxious for any letter with a Vermont return address. She sifted through the bills, magazines, and junk mail stuffed in our mailbox.

Nothing.

One day I retrieved the mail while Casey took Igor for a walk, and there in the mailbox was an envelope from Bennington College, but it was a thin one. Weren't they for rejections?

My heart sank. I couldn't bear the thought of her ripping open the envelope only to have her hopes dashed. Erika was puttering in the kitchen when I walked in and set the mail on the counter.

"Guess what?" I held up the envelope for her to see.

Erika turned around. "Oh my God. She got the decision!"

"Yeah, but it's a thin envelope. That's not good." I held up the envelope to the light but couldn't decipher a thing.

Erika scowled at me. "Don't say that. You don't know for sure." She took it from me and examined it, equally mystified by its contents.

As we passed it back and forth, Casey bounded through the front door with Igor in tow, both of them in a flurry of excitement. I held the envelope up for Casey to see. Her jaw dropped and she snatched it from my hand.

The moment of truth.

"Careful, don't rip it," Erika said. We stood together, jostling to get a view. Casey tore open the envelope and unfolded the letter while the envelope fluttered to the floor. A huge smile formed on her face as she read aloud in her high voice.

*"Dear Casey,*

*"Congratulations! On behalf of the students, the faculty and the staff it is my pleasure to offer you a place in the class of 2012 at Bennington College."*

She threw the letter up in the air and let out a whoop. We did high fives, hugs, and yelps of joy. I'd never seen her so happy with herself. She deserved it. She got her wish—her dream school. Erika and I were immensely proud and happy for her.

A whole new exciting life lay ahead.

———

With the pressure of college admission out of the way, each of us had settled into a comfortable groove. Casey practically marked the days off on her wall.

She would turn eighteen in May, less than five months away, and then in August she'd be off to Vermont. She rarely missed an opportunity to remind us of it, but she seemed to forget, or ignore, that we would continue to underwrite her lifestyle for another four years. We weren't completely out of the picture yet.

Soon after Casey's acceptance to Bennington, my mother flew out from Connecticut to see us over winter break. Casey and Mom adored each other. Mom was the perfect devoted grandmother to her only granddaughter, who could do no wrong. I was perfectly happy to perpetuate that story line just for peace of mind. We spent a night at an oceanside inn in Mendocino, stopped at an Anderson Valley winery on our way home, and took her for dim sum in San Francisco before settling down for Christmas. Casey practically fainted over the present my mother gave her—an iPhone.

By early January, my mother had returned home. After sixteen years as a stay-at-home mom, Erika left the house for a new job as a phlebotomist. Gray skies and soggy winter storms hammered the Bay Area, and we were only too happy to stay indoors and hibernate, until one evening over the Martin Luther King, Jr., Day weekend.

Several of Casey's friends had formed a bluegrass band called the Itchy Mountain Men. They developed quite a following, landing gigs, performing on the radio, and even cutting a CD. Casey considered herself a groupie.

They had a gig at Old St. Hilary's Church in Tiburon. Built in 1888, a good century before that finger of land became populated with multimillion-dollar homes, it was a simple Carpenter Gothic–style chapel that seated about a hundred people.

They were to play on Saturday, and Casey spent most of the afternoon obsessing over how best to doll herself up for a special night out. Her floor was littered with outfits. She summoned Erika—who was suffering from a virus—for help, only to banish her moments later when she couldn't magically make Casey look "gorgeous enough." Casey called off the entire evening, dissolving into tears in her room, and then pulled herself back together.

The show started at 9:00 and it was 8:15. She was supposed to be picked up by her girlfriends at 8:30. The last fifteen minutes were a frantic rush to finish up hair, makeup, and the third outfit, which was also the first outfit—the usual tomato-colored quilted hoodie, skinny jeans, suede boots, and a touch of Eau de Parfum.

At 8:25, Casey's tears were gone, and she was happy, ready, and waiting by the front door for her ride. Then she blurted out, "You guys should come!"

We were taken aback. For so long Casey had fought to distance herself from us. Erika was too sick to leave the house. I was thrilled to be invited, but what was the protocol? Should I pretend not to know her?

"Dad, you'll have to take a separate car."

I was still happy to accept her invitation. "Of course, honey."

Old St. Hilary's was full to capacity by the time I arrived. Body heat generated more than sufficient warmth on that cold

January night. The air in the chapel was thick and noisy with anticipation as I made my way from the front door to the end of the pews where I hoped to find a seat. I saw familiar faces in the crowd from church or school, all the way back to Casey's kindergarten class.

I took a seat where I could see the stage and peer over the people in front of me to look for Casey. I caught her at the foot of the stage with her girlfriends, chatting contentedly, falling into them and laughing. It was heartening to see her so genuinely happy. But I was afraid she'd see me, so I ducked down. I didn't want to embarrass her in front of her friends.

Hidden by the people in front of me, I watched as she broke off her conversation, turned around, and craned her neck in my direction. She spotted me in the crowd, lit up, and didn't hide her face. Instead she waved excitedly in my direction.

I must have been starved for her affection like a lovesick boy, because all I could think about was that she'd acknowledged me. I contemplated for a moment the years of fighting, the ugliness, the crying, the worrying, and the hurtful words. But all she had to do was acknowledge my existence as her dad in a crowd and I'd forget everything.

She'd be fine.

I felt like the luckiest guy in the world.

# NINETEEN

In the days following that horrific morning in January 2008—just weeks after the concert at Old St. Hilary's—I'd become obsessed with a single question:

*Why?*

I drifted through each day and went to bed each night thinking about her, torturing myself with guilt, drowning in soul-crushing grief. Sometimes, as if a protective mechanism in my brain had kicked in, I imagined that this was all a dream. I'd wake up to find her asleep in her room. Then I'd suffer a jolt to the chest.

The Coast Guard called off the search for her body after just two days; something about the currents being too strong—the ocean would be Casey's grave.

I felt a reflexive gag as I wrote her obituary.

I endlessly relived and dissected the events of the weekend before her death. Erika and I had both been fighting with Casey, starting with something seemingly trivial—a rude remark or refusal to clean up after herself; I hardly even remember. Things spun out of control. As tension mounted between us, Casey had spat out, *"Asshole! Motherfucker!"* She threatened to run away and live on the streets.

And my response? I got in her face and yelled at her like a drill sergeant, *"Good! Go ahead!"* I slammed her door, leaving her alone in her room, sobbing convulsively.

Later that night, I passed through the living room on my way to bed. She sat curled up on the sofa, staring hard at the TV, her eyes red and swollen from crying. We exchanged frosty glances.

And that was the last time I saw her.

———

That last ugly exchange screamed through my head. If I hadn't yelled at her, she might not have been so upset. If I hadn't ignored her on my way to bed, I might have thought twice, taken back my harsh words, and told her I didn't mean those nasty things. If I hadn't slept that extra half hour the next morning, I might have gotten to her room sooner, seen the note, and alerted the police in time.

But I did none of those things.

We'd had knock-down, drag-out fights since Casey was in grade school and they never ended in a catastrophe like this. She'd usually stomp off to her room. There were no clues that weekend that could have shed light on how she'd shifted so suddenly from "infuriated at Dad" to suicidal.

———

Some people suspected that drugs had played a role in Casey's suicide, but Erika and I had doubts. Despite our numerous busts, we'd never seen her out-of-control stoned or drunk, and she'd never been to rehab. She wasn't on any prescription medication at the time and wasn't out partying Monday night. Early Tuesday morning, she managed to drive the Saab to the bridge. The last video images captured her smoking a cigarette and jogging out onto the pedestrian walkway—not exactly the kind of behavior I'd associate with someone high on drugs. She easily climbed over that four-foot railing and, according to the police report, stood for ten to fifteen seconds before stepping off to her death. What could have gone through her mind in those crucial seconds before she made that fatal choice?

———

Casey's friends were as shell-shocked as we were. After her memorial service at St. Stephen's Church in Belvedere, an event that drew an overflow crowd, there was a reception in the parish hall. It was an awkward affair, with other parents struggling for words. It seemed we'd become separated by a glass wall. Was it pity, empathy, judgment, or terror that was in their faces? We couldn't tell. Perhaps the suicide of a child was just too toxic for people to handle. It raised the horrifying specter of contagion.

As the adults drifted away, Casey's friends circled around us. The collateral damage from her death was etched into their faces. They seemed to be looking for something from us. Perhaps they wanted to talk.

"Do you guys know anything about why she did it?" I asked.

They shook their heads and mumbled a collective "No."

Why would she have kept her closest friends in the dark? "I don't get it. She was so close to freedom. I thought that's what she wanted."

Everyone stared at the floor until her friend Julian spoke. "I don't think that Casey had any intention of going to Bennington."

Erika and I exchanged startled glances. "What makes you say that?" I asked.

"It's hard to explain," he said. "I think she just wanted to prove to herself and everyone else that she could get in."

Julian made an interesting point. But why would someone get what they wanted and then throw it all away?

———

After the memorial, we learned that Casey had chatted online late that Monday night with two childhood friends, Carly and Maryse.

Casey and Carly, both procrastinators, commiserated about deadlines for school projects they hadn't yet started. Later, Casey and Maryse griped about how much they hated school and about getting together over February break.

It began as a typical late-night talk that took an unusual turn. Casey talked about how lucky they were to live in Marin and then asked Maryse if she believed in reincarnation, claiming that she would probably be reincarnated into something *really shitty*. Within six hours of that conversation, Casey was dead.

———

I searched for more clues on her laptop, a hand-me-down gift from Erika and me for her sixteenth birthday. Most of the documents were homework assignments—an essay about a boy named Andrew titled "Andrew Is a Boring Fuck," some research articles she had pulled off the Web for A.P. History, a report on a book about the Depression that she had borrowed from me, the paper on the Eiffel Tower I edited for her that she claimed to have deleted, then ripped up and pieced back together. Almost no personal things, such as diaries, letters, or photographs. It was as if she'd made sure to eliminate anything that could have helped us understand what she was thinking, removing every trace of her emotional life.

I used one of her friends' passwords to get onto her Facebook page. Feeling like a voyeur reading what I wasn't supposed to see, I looked at her profile:

*About Me: Acts paradoxically; hugs trees; could out-sarcastic you.* Casey had a jagged wit. She was the master of the bitter jibe or cutting remark in a very *Seinfeld*-esque kind of way.

*Interested in: Men.* Since she was in middle school, we'd suspected that she'd never had a boyfriend nor, to our knowledge, any sexual encounter beyond maybe a kiss. It seemed so unusual for such a beautiful girl.

*Religious Views: Atheist without the negative connotations.* In Casey's mind, there was no God watching over her.

I was stunned to find dozens of pictures of Casey in the Photos section that I'd never seen. There was Casey hamming it up, dancing, smoking, and drinking beer at a party we weren't supposed to know about. In another photo, she sat in a lush meadow wearing a sleeveless black slip dress and flip-flops, the deep green of the tall grass around her standing in stark contrast to her blond hair and pale skin.

One series of pictures showed her walking through graffiti-covered cement batteries from World War II in the Marin Headlands. They reminded me of the abandoned buildings and cemeteries my friends and I sought for quirky photo shoots when we were her age.

There were photographs of Casey dressed in a short-sleeved dark purple dress and worn, untied Keds walking pensively around an abandoned construction site for some gaudy mansion in Belvedere. In the distance, the red towers of the Golden Gate Bridge were visible.

On her Facebook wall, she and her friends talked about homework, weekend plans, people they hated, their despicable parents, along with some reefer and random trash talk.

*Duuude, fuck me and my busy shittyness, where do you want to go to lunch on Thursday?*

*Your comments to Julian are way sketch.*

*Yo, Niggah, wanna chill tonight?*

I hit the Wall-to-Wall feature so I could read Casey's responses to her friends' posts:

*I don't get along with my mother at ALL. We are the same or opposites. I can't decide.* I'd often thought the source of their friction was the fact that both were so much alike—stubborn and argumentative.

*On the 26th my parents will be gone. Dude you should come over here and smoke cigarettes.* That was her reference to the overnight trip Erika and I took out of town after Christmas when she asked permission for "a few" friends to come over.

*I might get kicked out of the house when I turn 18 'cause my crying bothers my parents a lot.* Did her friends even know about her tantrums?

———

A tip from her friend Roxanne led to another secret online destination, a social networking site predating Facebook where we found heartbreaking journal posts dating back to 2005, when Casey was fourteen.

February 2005: *My body is sort of a benign tumor. I believe that is why I'm so terrified of relationships.*

April 2007: *I never let anyone get too close. I want someone to fix me, to hold me, tell me they love me with all my imperfections. I'm hopelessly flawed.*

October 2007, just four months before her suicide: *I've been failing for five years now. Five fucking years. Good job Casey, good*

*fucking job. What should I put on my college application? "Extremely
adept at killing myself slowly?"*

Casey had spat venom at us many times in fits of rage. But
they were the remarks of a petulant teenager who wanted to rattle
her parents. These online journal posts were private. They chilled
me as I read them.

There was still more.

———

Erika kept Casey's iPhone close by so she could listen to her voice
on the mailbox greeting: *"Please leave your message for . . . Quasey."*

On Valentine's Day, two weeks after Casey died, we picked
in silence at a plate of unheated pasta in the kitchen, left behind
by well-wishers, when Casey's phone hummed. Erika grabbed it,
trembling as she looked at the screen. There was a text string from
a girl named Rose.

*Casey are you there?*

*Casey are you all right?*

*Casey, what's going on? Isabel and I are starting to worry about
you.*

"I'm going to text her back." Erika punched at the screen
with her thumbs. "I don't know who she is, but she obviously
doesn't know what happened."

Within seconds the phone erupted with a gangster-rap ring-
tone. Erika picked it up. "Hello?"

Her expression turned from curious to somber. She put her
hand to her mouth and abruptly left the kitchen. After a half
hour she returned to place the phone back on the countertop.
Her face was ashen, as if she was in shock.

I spoke up. "Honey, what happened?"

Erika explained. Rose was at a boarding school in Michigan and had met Casey through another online message board when they were both in middle school. They talked openly and anonymously about depression, substance abuse, eating disorders, cutting, and suicidal thoughts. They'd connected regularly with a circle of girls from as far away as Texas, Pennsylvania, the U.K., Norway, and Brazil.

According to Rose, many of them were estranged from their parents, lonely and misunderstood, often self-destructive. It was in the safety of this online forum that Casey opened up about her own battles with demons and despair.

We learned that she'd driven the Saab to the Golden Gate Bridge late on January 27, the Sunday night before she died, apparently intent on jumping.

Listening to Erika's words, I felt as though I'd been smashed in the face by a two-by-four. My throat tightened as the story unfolded. Images of how it might have played out consumed me.

I pictured her parking the Saab in the Dillingham parking lot on the southbound side of the Highway 101 approach, taking the rickety wooden stairs to the pedestrian walkway under the bridge so that she could get to the northbound side facing views of the city and the bay.

Even late on a Sunday night she would have heard the *br-brapp, br-brapp* drone of traffic hitting the ribbed joints of the roadbed overhead. Then she would have climbed the stairs to the parking lot at Vista Point where the tourist buses stopped and maybe lit up a Camel Light, just as she did the following Tuesday morning. Then she would have headed for the pedestrian walkway that led onto the bridge.

A cautionary poster attached to the gate reads:

SEE SOMETHING? SAY SOMETHING!

A blue sign mounted over a yellow call box announces:

CRISIS COUNSELING. THERE IS HOPE. MAKE THE
CALL. THE CONSEQUENCES OF JUMPING FROM
THIS BRIDGE ARE FATAL AND TRAGIC!

But it wasn't the warning signs that stopped her. The six-
and-a-half-foot gate to the walkway had automatically closed and
locked at nine o'clock that night; it would reopen again at five
o'clock the next morning. So Casey returned to the Saab and
drove home.

Stunned, I asked Erika, "How did Rose know this?"

"She said that Casey reported the whole thing on the message
board after she came home." She held up Casey's iPhone with the
message from Rose for me to see.

> I had a really bad scare last night. It was so close between
> life and death.
> I'm not sure if I made the right decision. I'm just so tired of
> life and everything in it.
> I hope I never even think of doing such a thing again.
> :l :l :l

I stared at the words as if they'd been written by a stranger.

———

I'd always thought that if someone was bent on taking his or her
life, nothing would stop them. But I've since learned that suicide

is often impulsive—a transient urge. Once the impulse passed and the victim had an opportunity to reconsider, the chances were good that he or she wouldn't try again.

But Casey did try again. Less than thirty-six hours after she'd sent that text she went back. Her jump—her despair—had not been impulsive. There was something deeper.

# TWENTY

Three years later I remained haunted, just drifting through life. I lost my job when my division at Wells Fargo Bank was axed in the 2009 financial meltdown, but I didn't care about work or anything else anymore. I threw myself into writing Casey's story even though I'd never written a book before. In the spring of 2011, I sat in Dr. Palmer's office. I wanted to know what he'd learned in his sessions with Casey.

He was cordial but professionally detached, almost robotic. It was as if we were talking about any other patient rather than a dead child. I asked him what he remembered about Casey, anything that stood out. He flipped through his notes to jog his memory, as four years had passed since he'd seen her. Then his face brightened.

"I was impressed that she was a very bright kid with a piercing intelligence."

I nodded at his unexpectedly favorable opinion. *A piercing intelligence.*

He checked his notes again. "I remember asking her about her life when she was nine."

He explained that, in his experience, these were often a child's golden years, before the challenges and pressures of middle school and high school.

"She said that she was pretty happy then. She had a lot of friends, played soccer and video games, and she said she even had vivid dreams." He paused, studying his notepad. "She told me that was a pretty good time."

My mood lifted at the image of Casey sitting where I was, telling this bearded, professorial type about the good times in her life. It was gratifying to hear that we did something right. Life wasn't always miserable for her.

"That's nice to hear," I said. "What did she have to say about her high school years?"

"She talked about being irritable a lot of the time and she often had trouble sleeping." Perhaps noticing the concerned look on my face, he added, "She didn't like being irritable or angry, and she didn't necessarily blame it on you and Erika."

That was a pleasant surprise. "Really? She said that?" I asked. "I thought everything was our fault."

"She was actually quite unhappy that there was so much friction in her relationship with you." Dr. Palmer looked up from his pad. "She didn't like losing control of herself and she was even shocked by her own behavior sometimes."

I looked down at the floor, searching for another question as Dr. Palmer flipped back and forth through his notepad.

"I did ask her several times if she had any suicidal thoughts and she swore she didn't." He also reported that she'd insisted that she'd never used drugs, cut herself, or purged. I allowed myself a smirk. Casey was not about to divulge anything to an authority figure such as a parent or a shrink. I wondered if Dr. Palmer believed her denials or chose to avoid confrontation, but I said nothing.

"I'm afraid that's about all I've got," he said. We sat for a minute until he asked, "So how are *you* doing?"

His clinical demeanor remained unchanged. He was pleasant enough but I didn't sense an opening to spill my guts, so I swallowed the lump rising in my throat and mumbled, "Not very well," without elaborating. This wasn't a therapy session and he wasn't offering a salve for the pain. Nonetheless, our short meeting yielded some important information about how Casey saw herself and how she might've felt about her relationship with Erika and me. If only she'd had a bit more patience, Dr. Palmer might have found that magic pill she so desperately needed.

———

The following week, Erika and I met in Dianne's office. We sat across from her in the same oversize black leather chairs that seemed so comfortable years earlier when we'd first met. But this time there was an awkward tension between us.

I leaned forward so that I was at eye level with her. "You were Casey's last therapist. What did you see in her? What did you talk about?"

She prefaced her remarks with an outline of her therapy style—getting to know the patient, gaining their trust and connecting as a precondition to doing the work. She emphasized that in her forty years of practice, the overwhelming majority of her young patients had thoroughly embraced her. Then she drew a sharp distinction with Casey, describing her as bright and bored, but also exhibiting behavior typical of someone into drugs—sardonic, sarcastic, and disdainful of authority figures.

As I listened I couldn't help but think that this could have described any teenager, and I was irritated at her attempt to single out Casey from her other patients as if she were some kind of bad apple.

Erika and I exchanged scornful glances. I searched for a way to redirect the conversation. Dianne had mentioned something a while back about Casey's infancy, but I couldn't remember the term she'd used. In my foggy state my thought bubble vanished before I could decipher it. "Did you ever talk to her about her infancy or any memories she might've had about the orphanage?"

"Well, when I asked her to go to 'that place,' she'd scream at me."

None of this was helpful, so I tried yet another track. "Dianne, why do you think Casey jumped?"

She stiffened. "It was the drugs."

I was weary over her incessant drumbeat about drugs and spoke up. "I disagree, Dianne."

Casey was hardly a meth addict. Her drug use wasn't much different from that of many Marin County teenagers acting out or, in her case, a teenager trying to escape intolerable feelings. Unfortunately, Marin's rock 'n' roll hot tub legacy was well known, infecting younger generations with a blasé attitude toward under-age drinking and weed. Wild parties at absent parents' homes had been regularly written about in the local press. I didn't excuse or minimize teenage drug use as something entirely benign, but for her therapist to say that it drove her to suicide struck me as an attitude straight out of the 1930s movie *Reefer Madness*.

Lots of people who did drugs didn't kill themselves.

Apparently taken aback by my challenge, Dianne said, "Well, they weren't helpful. They may have confused her and distorted her ability to make rational decisions."

We sat in awkward silence until Dianne continued. "I think she saw me only as a doorway to medication."

I bristled at the picture Dianne painted of Casey, even in death, as some kind of crazed drug addict, but kept quiet. Erika broke the tension with some small talk until I glanced at my watch and announced that we should be on our way. "Thanks so much for your time, Dianne. This has been really helpful."

I kept my true thoughts to myself.

As we stood to go, Dianne said, "Take good care of yourselves. You can talk to me anytime." We gave each other hugs that felt somewhat more artificial than they did when we arrived. We walked through her cramped waiting room to the hallway. I turned to Erika. "What did you make of that?"

She rolled her eyes. Her expression said everything.

"Right." I nodded.

We didn't even bother to bring up the *Social Intelligence* book or ask why Dianne had recommended it. At that point, it was just another waste of time.

# TWENTY-ONE

A man receives only what he is ready to receive, whether physically or intellectually or morally, as animals conceive at certain seasons their kind only. We hear and apprehend only what we already half know . . . Every man thus tracks himself through life, in all his hearing and reading and observation and travelling. His observations make a chain. The phenomenon or fact that cannot in any wise be linked with the rest of what he has observed, he does not observe. By and by we may be ready to receive what we cannot receive now.

—Henry David Thoreau

I had the first draft of Casey's story finished by the time I'd met with Dr. Palmer and Dianne. Other than recounting Erika's and my journey to Poland, there were only glancing references to and speculation about the effects on Casey's behavior of her abandonment and adoption. They were never pursued or treated seriously, even after Dianne had raised the issue in passing. It just seemed inconceivable to me that Casey's infancy had anything to do with her later life and death. After all, I reasoned that I had no memory of my own life before the age of seven other than from photographs and home movies. How could she? But some people see clearly what others can't. They are too close to the subject.

I had been working with a group of memoir writers who convened weekly in the home of our writing coach at her stately yellow-and-white-trimmed Victorian home on the outskirts of Haight-Ashbury in San Francisco. It wasn't until our coach critiqued my draft that she found the story I had completely missed. It was that glancing reference Dianne made in our last meeting after Casey had quit therapy four years earlier, in the spring of 2007.

Attachment disorder.

I thought about Casey in her room, shutting us out with a battered, splintered door. In the years since her suicide it had been replaced with a new six-panel door painted a glossy white, in a vain attempt to paper over the memories of battles raging on either side. Across the hall there was a dimple on the wall that a splash of paint couldn't hide, the result of one of our fights. So many times I'd stood outside that door listening to her wailing and sobbing inside, helpless to console her. Once I'd opened the door, ignoring a photograph she'd posted on it of an oak tree, on which she'd written, *Entrez-Vous? Non!* It was French for "Keep Out!"

As soon as I walked in, she abruptly stopped, as if a needle had been lifted from a record. She fixed me with a hard stare but her mouth quivered.

"Get out."

I paused for a moment, searching for something to say, some

way to connect. "Honey . . ." Once again, I couldn't find the words quickly enough.

"OUT!"

My face burned with humiliation as I retreated.

The minute I was back in the hallway and shut the door, the awful howling resumed. It was a cry for help. But when help came, she refused it and slammed the door.

*Why?*

Now, years later, inside her room, taped to the hutch on her desk was a piece of crinkled computer paper with a message in red crayon, all in capital letters, the awkward, uneven creation of a five-year-old Casey.

DEAR MOM AND DAD
I LOVE YOU AND MISS YOU BUT I DON'T HATE YOU
BY CASEY

There was an overstuffed pencil holder emblazoned with the Japanese cartoon character Domo, which sported its trademark angry, toothy snarl that American girls found so impossibly cute. Erika had taken a Father's Day card that Casey had made when she was thirteen and propped it against Domo. In her distinctive, left-handed curly scrawl, Casey wrote:

*You sir (yes, you!) have been \*NOMINATED\* to receive . . .*
THE BEST DAD AWARD!

I ♥ U!
*I hope you enjoy this card written, produced, directed*
*and pretty much made by me.*
*U are the best dad ever!*

Her black IKEA bed was in the corner of the room with the *Trainspotting* poster overhead. There was an inscription at the bottom in bold letters that was tragically ironic:

CHOOSE YOUR FUTURE.
CHOOSE LIFE.

Her bed was a mountain of pillows. She liked to cocoon herself. But she was never the sentimental type, never into dolls, never into collecting things, other than her Beanie Babies and Pokémon cards (she thought they'd be worth a fortune someday). Though she had plenty of stuffed animals, such as plush pink Piggy, Toucan, and big old Pooh Bear, she didn't have a favorite to drag around and hug in bed at night as I did.

Her only constant companion was her comfort pillow from Poland. Erika had it restuffed and re-covered many times over the years, and had propped it neatly against the headboard.

———

I sat in my home office in front of my computer and Googled *attachment disorder.* The first hit brought me to Wikipedia:

Attachment disorder is a disorder of *mood, behavior,* and *social relationships* arising from a failure to form normal attachments to primary caregivers in early childhood. Such a failure would result from unusual early experiences of neglect, *abuse,* or abrupt separation from caregivers in the first three years of life.

Then I searched a related term, *reactive attachment disorder,* or *RAD*:

Children with RAD are presumed to have grossly disturbed internal working models of relationships, which may lead to interpersonal and behavioral difficulties in later life. There are few studies of long-term effects, but the opening of orphanages in Eastern Europe in the early 1990s provided opportunities for research on infants and toddlers brought up in very deprived conditions.

"Orphanages in Eastern Europe in the early 1990s." This couldn't have been just Romania. It was the Czech Republic, Slovakia, Hungary, Bulgaria, and Poland. I searched and sifted through mounds of data and studies from sources ranging from attachment experts and clinicians to blog posts by adoptive parents. A behavioral profile of the adopted child began to emerge.

Emotional Regulation: Because of the absence of the modulating influence of a dedicated caregiver in infancy, the adopted child frequently has a low tolerance for frustration, ineffective coping skills and impulse control, and trouble self-soothing. She can be clingy, hyperreactive, quick to anger or bursting into tears over what others might consider insignificant or nonexistent slights. It can be difficult to calm her with logic or discipline. She may have out-of-control, prolonged tantrums long past toddlerhood that are disproportionate to circumstances, giving the appearance of emotional immaturity.

Control: Abandoned in infancy, the adopted child has learned early not to trust. Controlling her environment and distancing others around her—especially caregivers—become paramount as a way to protect herself from further abandonment. This can affect her social realm, where she must navigate relationships and read social cues. She may feel threatened by others, have trouble tolerating relationships or participating in competitive games other than on her own terms. She can be a sore loser when things don't go her way. She may have trouble sharing toys, food, or friends, long past what is age-appropriate. She may lack cause-and-effect thinking and blame others for her mistakes. Convinced perhaps that caregivers are unavailable and untrustworthy, she might avoid asking for help. She might be seen as bossy, but not to everyone. She can be manipulative—extremely charming, in fact, even indiscriminately affectionate, toward strangers—but cool and remote at home.

Transitions: Because of her need for control, the adopted child can have difficulties with transitions, especially when they come unexpectedly. She can't easily "go with the flow." Rather, she does best in environments of structure, predictability, and regularity. Changes in routine—such as transitions from the school year to summer, vacations, and holidays—are times of great stress and acting out.

Discipline: Trust, control, and discipline go hand in hand for the adopted child. She may display a pattern of disobedient, defiant, and hostile behavior toward authority figures that goes beyond the norm, giving the appearance of being unduly stubborn and strong-willed. Epic battles can erupt over the most trivial things.

Self-Image: The adopted child whose needs are not met in infancy builds up a pessimistic and hopeless view of herself, her family, and society. She may be uncomfortable with physical closeness or intimacy. She can hear compliments from parents yet feel no association. She's not worthy of love or respect, and may have enclosed her heart in a vault and fought to deny access to anyone who truly loves her. "I love you" can strike terror in her heart. She can't feel love, believes that it hurts, and wants nothing of it. She may manifest destructive behaviors such as self-mutilation, eating disorders, and suicidal tendencies.

A simple Google search explained everything about Casey. The uncontrollable tantrums and crying jags. Her lack of patience, whether waiting an extra minute in her high chair for some ice cream or, years later, learning to skate or snowboard. Her tendency to be thin-skinned at home with no tolerance for the most benign joke or jab aimed at her. And my reaction to this? Out of sheer frustration, I told her to stop crying, grow up, and act her age.

Great job, Dad.

She didn't handle threesomes well and would stomp home in tears from a friend's house feeling left out or slighted, losing it when something didn't go her way. I remembered our earliest meeting with Dr. Klein, when we probed him for an opinion about her bossiness and combativeness, but he described an entirely different child at school—a delight in the classroom who rarely had to be reprimanded.

Power struggles erupted over the most ridiculous things— *Casey, please put your dirty dish in the sink; Casey, please don't leave your wet towel on the bathroom floor; Casey, please take Igor for a walk.* We were stuck in a never-ending cycle of time-outs, withheld privileges, abandoned reward programs, groundings, and empty threats to spend her college fund on a year in purgatory. We resorted to spanking her, even threatening to hit her, violating every tenet of good parenting and giving her more reason to despise us.

And transitions? Maybe Bennington was the last straw. I thought about Julian's theory at the memorial that Casey had no intention of going; she just wanted to prove a point. For all of her bluster about Bennington, I could see how she could have been terrified. She was a creature of habit, had never been away by herself (except for the Alaska trip), never shared a bedroom or bathroom. At home, she had some measure of safety and privacy where she could unleash her rages and tantrums without fear of repercussions. At school, there would be no place to hide and unload in private. She'd be vulnerable, exposed.

Her issues with self-image went far beyond teenage angst. She seemed to loathe herself. But in retrospect, it was almost impossible to distinguish among the typical insecurities of a teenager, attachment issues from infancy, and dangerous suicidal tendencies when the symptoms looked so much alike. It would be impossible to treat every raging, sullen teen moping around the house as a potential suicide risk.

I had stumbled onto something big almost by accident, something that had been staring us in the face for years, and everyone had been blind to it. Casey was alone, in pain and unable to trust, and we couldn't see it. In her fragile state, there wasn't enough to live for, not enough for her to stay in the game, to see through the rough patches. Her perception of the future was bleak, hopeless.

Casey must have had some kind of an attachment disorder.

# TWENTY-TWO

I scoured the Marin County library and the Internet for every book and article I could find on attachment. I contacted experts on adoption and attachment issues. Several of them agreed to talk to me about the disorder and what was being done to help the children and their parents. Nearly all of the experts were either adoptive parents who struck out on their own as I did, or were adoptees trying to understand themselves.

I learned that attachment begins with the trusting bond formed between a child and mother or other primary caregiver during infancy. This bond becomes the blueprint for all future relationships. The British psychiatrist John Bowlby, widely considered to be the founding father of attachment theory, says that at birth a baby cannot automatically self-regulate. Her emotional state is as simple as stressed or not stressed. When she is stressed—from hunger, a wet diaper, insufficient sleep, or fear—she cries. She is brought back into balance when the caregiver responds with soothing sounds, gentle touch, and loving looks.

Nancy Newton Verrier, an adoption specialist in Lafayette, California, provided me with her own analogy of mother-child separation. "It's very unnatural to separate babies and mothers," she said. "You can't adopt a kitten or puppy for about eight weeks, in order to give the babies time to wean off their mothers, but we give away human babies to strangers as early as birth." I never thought of it that way, and yet it seemed so obvious. Why would we treat animals with more deference than humans?

An infant left alone, with no instinctive soothing mechanism, lives in a state of prolonged fear and hyperarousal. Unable to summon help or physically escape, the infant's only protection from this unendurable state is to emotionally withdraw.

Amy Klatzkin is a marriage and family therapist intern I met with at the Child Trauma Research Center at UCSF/San Francisco General Hospital. She is also an adoptive mother.

"There's only one thing worse than an abusive relationship, even if it's harmful," she said. "And that's no relationship at all, just nothingness."

I saw Casey alone in her crib in the orphanage as Amy continued. "Casey was probably getting sustenance but no connection, not even a tiny attachment. People come and go, and you never know if they'll be back. They're all equally distant and interchangeable to her."

She went on to talk about another kind of separation—the moment the child left the orphanage system with her adoptive parents. There was an element of predictability left behind—familiar sensations, sounds, and smells—for something unknown with two complete strangers. To ease that separation, Ms. Klatzkin offered a good piece of advice: leave the child in her clothes from the orphanage, even if they're dirty or smelly. "Let them have some continuity," she said. "It's our instinct to cling."

In *High Risk: Children Without a Conscience*, the clinical psychologists Ken Magid and Carole McKelvey wrote: "If a child does not form a loving bond with the mother, she does not develop an attachment to the rest of mankind, and literally does not have a stake in humanity. Incomprehensible pain is forever locked in her soul because of the abandonment she suffered as an infant."

Incomprehensible pain. My daughter. The awful wailing behind her door.

So profound is the effect of institutionalization that Dr. Jerri Ann Jenista, a pediatrician and writer in the field of adoption medical health, suggests that *all* institutionalized orphans be considered at risk for attachment issues.

The longer they stay in the institution, the greater the damage. "We now know that if the child is adopted within the first year, the adverse effects of institutionalization are not too difficult to treat," explained Dr. Robert Marvin, the director of the Mary D. Ainsworth Child-Parent Attachment Clinic at the University of Virginia Medical Center. "But for a child like Casey, adopted at fourteen months, there's already been a fair amount of psychological and brain developmental damage that leads to very unusual behavior." In fact, studies have shown that institutionalized children have measurably different brain structures from those raised in a family. Researchers have found striking abnormalities in tissues that transmit electrical messages across the brain, perhaps explaining some of the dysfunctions seen in neglected and orphaned children.

The effects of institutionalization rarely go away. Parents of these kids find that depression, moodiness, self-mutilation, screaming fits, defiance, and academic struggles can be "normal" parts of life. Some children leave home and break contact with their adoptive families. Job instability, unplanned pregnancies, suicide attempts, and stints in disciplinary, rehab, and psychiatric programs are not uncommon.

Patricia, the adoptive mother of a boy from southern Poland, wrote to me that her son—then an eight-year-old—was at the emotional level of a five-year-old. Though he had recovered from early developmental delays, he was still prone to meltdowns, anxiety attacks, and struggles with self-esteem.

An adoptive mother of a girl from northwestern Russia wrote that her daughter was born to alcoholic parents and was unschooled and neglected until she was placed for adoption at age seven. Her adoptive mother received her at age eleven with a range of challenges, from growth deficiencies to language delays and learning disabilities. At the age of eighteen, she had the emotional maturity of a nine-year-old. The slightest provocation could send her into a rage or sobbing fit. Her parents feared that she couldn't be trusted on her own.

Of course, this is, for many parents, only part of the story. As one mother wrote about her troubled daughter from Russia, "She has brought more love into my life than I ever thought possible."

My reaction to these difficult stories was envy. Their children were still alive. My daughter was dead. I had failed in my first duty as a father, to keep her safe. The information I needed to keep her alive was out there, but it was just beyond my reach. It was in the library and on the Internet.

I had never thought to look.

# TWENTY-THREE

If we could turn back the clock, there is so much that we would have done differently. Casey's life didn't have to end so abruptly and tragically.

I now see a very different person on the other side of that battered bedroom door. Not an angry, misbehaving teenager bent on tormenting her parents, but a child suffering unfathomable pain for whom comfort was out of reach.

She tried to speak to us but couldn't get through. We couldn't hear her, couldn't understand her, or tuned her out as the decibels rose. Likewise, we tried to speak to her, but our words never reached her. Erika and I were desperate to love her but she had trouble letting us in. We reacted to our communication void with frustration, shutting each other out. That was a fatal mistake whose consequences we couldn't possibly know. We had no idea how far out on a ledge Casey was.

On the surface, everything appeared normal; in fact, better than normal. She'd gotten into her dream school, yet that wasn't enough to dent the iceberg of agony that sat below the surface, that she kept hidden from everyone. Only occasionally did she give a hint of her true feelings. Her cries for help were too faint for people to hear, so she weighed the options—live in pain or choose death.

Erika and I were blind from the outset. I thought about the morning we picked Casey up from the orphanage. We were so intent on changing her into some nice, clean girlie clothes that it never dawned on us to ask if she had something she clutched in her crib—a pillow, a stuffed animal, a blanket? For all I know now, we'd left something behind that was indispensable to her, further compounding her distress. To ease the shock of this transition, we should have asked for an article of clothing, a plaything, something she might have snuggled with to keep her company and have something familiar to hold on to, but we didn't.

In their two books, *Adopting the Hurt Child* and *Parenting the Hurt Child*, Dr. Gregory Keck and Regina Kupecky note that adoptive parents want to believe that a sound attachment had formed with former caregivers, in a sort of turnkey process that was readily transferable to them. The adoption becomes a cure-all for the child's difficulties.

So it was for us, we thought. Overjoyed at her astonishing progress in our first few days together, camped out in a cramped hotel room in Warsaw, Erika and I became convinced that Casey wasn't a special needs child at all. She had just been understimulated in the orphanage; nothing that two loving parents couldn't fix. We were part of a fairy tale—two able-bodied Americans rescuing a Polish orphan from her caring but impoverished birth mother, who wanted a better life for her daughter.

We treated Casey as if she were our new pet. She was in good American hands. Just feed her, burp her, change her diaper, bounce her around, and park her in front of the TV when Mom and Dad need a rest. Then there were the outbursts.

I know now that adoptive parents who view their children's disruptive behavior as just normal growing pains are ignoring a time bomb. They need to distinguish between the physical and emotional age of their child and adapt their parenting expectations to the child's emotional age, that emotional immaturity I'd read about and, of course, had seen in Casey.

We should have had her assessed. Ray Kinney, a director and staff psychologist at Cornerstone Counseling Services in Wisconsin, spoke to me about the importance of assessment for children who have lived in orphanages. Having seen hundreds of deprived children over thirty-five years of clinical practice, he said that this was a crucial prerequisite to determining an appropriate intervention strategy.

That first night in the hotel room in Warsaw, when she was inconsolable, rocking herself to sleep, we just wanted her to quiet down so that we could get some rest. Instead of parking her in her stroller in front of a blaring TV—something she'd probably never seen before—we should have taken her into bed with us, held her and soothed her. If it were possible, we should have held her for our whole first month together without putting her down. Maybe we would have had a different result. What she needed then was lots of human touch.

From the moment we brought Casey into our home, it seemed as though we did everything wrong. We assumed that the past would fade into oblivion; nurture would prevail over nature. We took our parenting cues from the pop culture experts.

As a toddler, we tried to teach Casey manners, patience, and independence. When she acted out inappropriately and threw temper tantrums, we scolded and punished her. But we failed to see what was at the root of her outbursts, and our reactions only made matters worse. Rather than sending her off by herself, we should have stayed with her, helped her calm down and self-soothe. She needed to know that Mom and Dad would always be there for her unconditionally.

When Casey entered school, we were mystified by what appeared to be a split personality—a perfect angel at school and a defiant, immature brat at home. We consulted family, friends, teachers, and guidance counselors, and were told that Casey was strong-willed and a bit high-strung; she'd grow out of it.

Erika and I felt that we were the problem. We spoiled her. We were inconsistent. We needed to be tougher with her. So we read books such as *Raising Your Spirited Child*, tried reward systems and used TV, the computer, and playdates as leverage for good behavior. We blamed each other for our lousy parenting skills and our inability to get our daughter to mind her parents like everyone else's kids did. We didn't realize that the provocation and aggression we saw in her may have been caused by her anxiety about further rejection, something she may not have understood herself.

Nancy Verrier told me that the adopted child can push for rejection even though that's the opposite of what she wants. She constantly tests her parents to see if they'll reject her, just to get the inevitable over with. As she tests her parents' commitment, often playing into their own insecurities about being good enough, the parents become defensive and retaliatory instead of understanding and steadfast. Their reactions can provoke the very outcome she feared in the first place—being sent to a residential treatment center or boarding school, or being kicked out onto the street.

———

A 2008 white paper, "Therapeutic Parenting," prepared by the Association for the Treatment and Training in the Attachment of Children (ATTACh), begins with the following message:

. . . Parenting a child who has a disorder of attachment is the hardest job you will ever have. . . . It requires you to give and give, without receiving much in return. . . . It requires rethinking your parenting instincts. . . . It means making conscious, therapeutic parenting decisions . . . [and having a] constant focus on the deeper meaning of your child's behavior, so that you respond to the causes, needs, and motivations of your child. It is exhausting. It is isolating, as family and friends tend to keep their distance, uncomfortable with the drama that surrounds these children.

Heather Forbes is an internationally published author and consultant, adoptive mother, and cofounder of the Beyond Consequences Institute in Boulder, Colorado. She said that her work is geared toward healing the parent-child relationship, with emphasis on the parents, because she believes that the child's healing process must come from them rather than the therapist. "Parents who are strong in who they are, even if the child is rejecting or defiant, don't have to take things personally and can love unconditionally."

Like the other experts I talked to, she urged parents to focus on the child's perspective rather than their own. What is driving my child's behavior? Why is she stressed out and acting this way? No matter how unpleasant the message, parents should give the child free rein to vent, because it's important for her to be heard. Good manners and appropriate language can be worked on later.

"All these kids feel like Casey," she told me. "Hopelessly flawed. They can't be fixed. These feelings never go away. It wasn't that you didn't love Casey; she just didn't get it the right way."

In the early 2000s, Dr. Marvin, along with several colleagues from the Marycliff Institute in Spokane, Washington, developed the "Circle of Security," a protocol to diagnose attachment disorder and design individualized intervention programs aimed at attachment-caregiving relationships for both toddlers and preschool children. The process, which takes place over twenty weekly group sessions, is designed to help parents gain a deeper understanding of their children and themselves, and to become more accurate and empathic in reading their children's complex and subtle cues—anger at a parent when the truth could be entirely different, or defiance masking an inability to adapt to a new routine. With a better understanding of their children's behavior, parents are shown how to apply more "user-friendly" attachment techniques.

"Our coaching helps parents shift their focus from stopping undesirable behavior to moving in to calm the child when she's out of control and can't self-soothe," Dr. Marvin explained. For example, instead of isolating the child as punishment for misbehavior, stay with her, acknowledge the upset, let her be herself. Sometimes, on some subconscious level, this behavior may be a reaction to her early abandonment. Adoptive parents need to understand and acknowledge that first loss.

"When parents follow that approach they start to see these behaviors decrease very quickly." He insisted that children, when distressed, respond much better to parents when they take charge and soothe rather than discipline, as one would a baby—the baby that child used to be and, in a way, still is.

Jane Brown is an adoption therapist in Ontario, Canada, who encourages adoptees to explore through playful group activities what it means to be adopted, how to build a self-concept as an adoptee, and how to be in the world. In a safe group, the children are more willing to take risks and model for one another, sometimes participating simply by listening and watching. She gives the youngsters exercises to encourage them to explore their beliefs about what happened to them, how they felt about their birth parents, why they'd adopted a baby, all in an attempt to lower their defenses and get their story out.

———

We'd spun tales about Casey's adoption from the very beginning. When she showed no curiosity about her past or birth family, we took her at her word. It never occurred to us that Casey's rages might've been rooted in suppressed feelings about her early abandonment. We tried to protect her from the pain of knowing about her stillborn twin, but maybe deep down she knew.

We looked at her birthdays through our eyes, not hers. They might have been yet another reminder of loss, not celebration. That would have explained her tendency to sabotage the entire occasion. It was probably Casey's instinct to run from strong emotions, but what she really needed was help from an understanding professional to piece together the narrative of her past and provide a healthier sense of herself as a whole person.

Ray Kinney claimed that, all too often, parents sugarcoat the adoption story to avoid inflicting more pain on their child. He takes a different approach—helping the child reconstruct her adoption story. She needs to know that her experience was real, and her constant and conflicting feelings about it are appropriate and legitimate. By getting the story out honestly—even if it isn't pretty—the child has a more complete sense of herself.

"They want the whole story, and when they hear it, maybe they can understand what it was like to be in their mother's shoes," he said. "When we let the child understand the trauma she's had, what happened to her as a baby, and how that's played out for her entire life, she can start to gain control over her emotions."

The onset of adolescence, middle school, and high school adds another layer of intensity into the mix. When Casey's tantrums became profanity-laced rages punctuated with *I hate you*, we tried to control her with endless groundings and withheld privileges until we admitted defeat. The fact that she seemed impervious to discipline we took as a personal failure. But her rages may have had little to do with us. Her inner existence was a toxic stew of fear, stress, loneliness, and self-hatred that she hinted at only on LiveJournal and the message board.

———

Dr. David Brodzinsky, a professor emeritus at Rutgers University, founding director of the Donaldson Adoption Institute, and a coauthor of the 1992 book *Being Adopted: The Lifelong Search for Self*, wrote about the effects of long-term institutionalization:

> For children placed early, the sense of loss emerges gradually as the child's cognitive understanding of adoption begins to unfold. For children adopted later, feelings of loss can be more traumatic and overt, particularly by middle school when the youngster begins to reflect on what it means to be adopted, perhaps associating it with feeling odd, different.
>
> At the extreme, resentment and rage against the adoptive parents may erupt from feelings of shame and guilt about who she is—unlovable—to which she may respond with destructive outbursts. As one adoptee said: *"Being chosen by your adoptive parents means nothing compared to being un-chosen by your birth mother."*

Dr. Brodzinsky cautions that there is a wide range in the expression of adoption-related grief, from only a slight recognition of pain to something more frequent and intense. Often the sense of loss can be masked by intense anger, denial, emotional distance, and exterior bravado. But beneath that tough suit of armor lies a child who has been deeply hurt by life. She is the most vulnerable and difficult to reach.

# TWENTY-FOUR

I began to understand what it might have felt like to be Casey—the baby screaming her outrage from her crib at being left behind, thrust into the arms of two strangers from a foreign country who couldn't comfort her no matter how well intentioned they were.

She despised them for their lack of understanding, and for being so foolish as to love someone like her. So she put on a show of bravado, suited up her armor, and pretended that she needed no one, especially them. But at the same time, she might have looked at her behavior—something she just hinted at with Dr. Palmer—and asked herself, "What the hell is wrong with me?"

She hid behind that suit of armor, lashing out at the only two people who were safe—her adoptive parents. I'd come to learn that parenting a child who had suffered so much trauma in infancy was completely counterintuitive. The time-tested methods of raising and disciplining a securely attached child that we'd learned from Dr. Spock, T. Berry Brazelton, and Dr. Phil were woefully inadequate for a child like Casey. "Sometimes you have to parent in a way that's good for your child even if it doesn't feel good to you," Ray Kinney said.

Dr. Keck recommended that infants shouldn't be left alone to "cry it out." As I'd heard from others, the parent should stay with her if she was screaming, crying, and inconsolable.

There was that disastrous trip to the Yerba Buena skating rink when Casey was eight. We left her alone in her room to cry it out because that's what she said she wanted. If we'd known better, we would have overridden her.

Erika could have rubbed her back and massaged her feet, cooing in a soft voice the way she did when Casey was younger, chanting a Polish verse that Casey loved as an infant. It was about a little spider sneaking up on her, crawling up her tummy. Erika learned it from her mother, and my mother had a similar verse, but instead of a spider it was a creeping mouse. I imagined Casey's face lighting up in anticipation of what was to come when Erika's fingers would pounce on her neck with the dreaded spider tickle, eliciting her delicious laugh: *Ha ha ha!*

Dr. Keck wrote that the child should be fed on demand to establish a pattern that her needs will be met and help her develop a sense of trust that relief is there when she's distressed. Day care was to be avoided, if possible, as it could reinforce the pattern of abandonment by the primary caregiver.

Thank God, we got one thing right.

We continued to send Casey to therapists who treated her as they did their other patients, repeatedly focusing on corrective behavior rather than getting to the core—until Casey had had enough.

Now I don't blame her. She was right. Their kind of therapy was a waste of time.

Unfortunately, in our blindness, Erika and I were enraged.

We saw this as just one more of her infuriating acts of defiance and our failure to control her. We didn't realize that she might have just given up on herself.

Children like Casey have to be treated differently—different therapies, different parenting—if they are to survive and thrive. The professionals to whom we'd dragged her over the years were not equipped to understand, deal with, or even recognize her unique life experience. They resorted to the only treatments they'd been taught. After all, they'd worked for their other young patients. Why not Casey?

A blog post titled "When Therapists Don't Get It," on a Bay Area adoption website, recounted the frustration of an adoptive mother seeking help for her son through traditional therapy channels. She reported that even therapists skilled at working with troubled children couldn't help and may have made matters worse. As I'd heard before, they focused on her son's undesirable behavior, as if correcting the symptoms would cure the disease.

She wrote: "Parents seek out experts because they want to help their child to be happy and emotionally healthy. To constantly go to therapists and be told that what is 'wrong' with their child is the parents' fault is infuriating. Finding a therapist who gets it is the key to helping everyone in the family."

I talked with Heather Forbes about our disappointments with therapists.

"Unfortunately, I hear stories like this all the time," she assured me. "If you don't get to that emotional place—the depth of the heart and soul where she felt rejected—you'll probably never have success."

There are thousands of public and private adoption agencies and attorneys available to prospective parents in the United States, but postadoption resources are sorely lacking. In the San

Francisco Bay Area, the fifth-largest metropolitan area in the United States, with more than eight million people and a large international adoption community, there are only a handful of specialized adoption therapists. I'd learned from my own quest that finding them is a challenge.

If only I could have found someone who truly understood Casey and connected with her in a way none of our therapists had, maybe she would have developed some trust and opened up. If Casey had been willing to participate in group therapy with other adopted teens, maybe she wouldn't have felt so alone, even if she did nothing more than listen. The few clues we found after her death suggested that she had searched for a community of similarly troubled teenagers. She wanted to connect with others. I talked at length with Jane Brown about her adopted daughter from China. When she was nine years old, her psychiatrist put her on a mood stabilizer to manage her violent mood swings. Within a week, the medication took the edge off her rages and her tantrums subsided. Once she was calm, the psychiatrist was able to work on her psychological and behavioral issues.

I'd looked at medication for Casey as a last resort, frightened of the potential side effects. Would things have turned out differently if we had introduced medication to her much earlier than seventeen?

"These kids are forever more vulnerable and reactive to stress, but they can learn to deal with it. Medication can help," Brown said. "Attachment can be a piece of the puzzle, but it may not be the whole puzzle."

There was another thing we did right—the cardinal rule I learned from Nancy Verrier—*never threaten abandonment*.

Not that we didn't think about sending Casey off to rehab or reform school, as other parents had. But my consideration at the time was more practical than altruistic; reform schools are every bit as expensive as elite private colleges.

Perhaps if we had mastered just one of the parenting techniques I'd learned about, or used every opportunity to remind her how much she mattered, or responded to *I'll kill myself if . . .* not with silence, but with an impassioned accounting of an empty world without her, we could have kept Casey alive.

This didn't have to happen.

Ray Kinney told me that the effects of institutionalization never completely disappear. "These kids can learn to not let those wounds control their lives."

Ultimately, Casey might have left home with better coping skills, a healthier self-image, and the confidence that she had two parents whom she could trust to be there whenever she needed them.

# TWENTY-FIVE

I thought back to those smiling faces and tearful goodbyes from the caregivers in the white lab coats at the orphanage in Mrągowo, and wondered what lay beyond that cheerful visitation room, the only room we saw.

In my search for answers to Casey's suicide, I'd Googled *Polish orphanages*. Perhaps there was more I could learn about the Dom Dziecka system and how it might have influenced the foundation of Casey's personality and emotional architecture. After several searches I found a treasure trove of information.

Agape Trust is a nonprofit organization that supports young adults in Poland who were raised in the state orphanage system. I sent an e-mail inquiry to the site and within a week was in contact with the couple in charge: Vic, a South African, and his Polish wife, a social worker named—ironically—Joanna, Casey's birth name.

Vic wrote that the Dom Dziecka orphanage system dated from the end of World War II when the country was left with an estimated one million war orphans. More than sixty years after the war, the system is far smaller, serving an estimated twenty-five thousand children, but the institutional structure still has a child-to-caregiver ratio as high as ten to one. The emotional needs of the children are often sacrificed in favor of basic care, in what amounts to a highly regimented, mass-care environment.

Staff members are discouraged from bonding with the children. It is considered to be unprofessional. But there are also practical considerations. Caregivers can be easily overwhelmed by so many children clamoring for their affection, leading to burnout. Their inability to respond effectively to the children's needs can further traumatize their charges.

When they leave the Dom Dziecka system, the vast majority of these children—many having suffered emotional trauma before they'd entered—are unprepared for life with their adoptive families. One article revealed that more than 90 percent of Polish orphans might have some form of attachment disorder.

Casey had been dealt a number of devastating blows before we'd even met. From the delivery room she went directly to an incubator where she stayed for two months with little human contact. Then she was sent to an orphanage where she lived for a year, well cared for but emotionally starved. She may have spent much of her young life lying in her crib in a room with other infants, listening to them fussing and crying until it was time for a feeding or diaper change, and lights out. She lost her mother, her sister, and any possible genetic link. She had no close relationship with a caregiver, no sense of safety and trust in the world she had been born into. I wonder if her birth mother ever held her before saying goodbye forever?

As Vic wrote in one of our e-mail exchanges, echoing what I'd heard from others: "Considering the fact that Casey had been emotionally traumatized as an infant, her subsequent behavior under those circumstances was perfectly normal."

Patricia, who wrote about the boy she adopted from southern Poland, said that he had been delivered to an orphanage at five months old. He stayed until he was two. Patricia had unusual access to the orphanage, and described a clean, production-line existence of ruthless efficiency. Caregivers were instructed to carry the children facing away from them to avoid attachment. Bath time reminded her of a car wash. Boys and girls—all under age five, lined up naked and crying—stepped into a tub where one caregiver soaped them up, one rinsed them down, one dried them off, and another dressed them in pajamas.

The mother of a boy from northeastern Bulgaria told me that she had adopted him at age three and a half from a shabby, Soviet-era orphanage that housed about 250 children. There was no outdoor play area, so the children often remained indoors. With coal for heating expensive and scarce, it wasn't unusual for the younger children to be confined to their cribs in the winter. Their meals consisted of lukewarm teas, soups, watery juice drinks, canned fruits, and breads. Potty breaks amounted to sitting on chamber pots out in the open; diapers were nonexistent. This woman's son is now in his early twenties, emotionally immature, prone to violent temper tantrums and depression. He has learning disabilities.

# TWENTY-SIX

I finally had questions. Where could I find answers?

My first overture was to a group that promoted Polish adoptions and organized regular social events for adoptees and their families in the United States. With my e-mail exchange from Vic about the Dom Dziecka orphanage system fresh in my mind, I felt that this group would be understanding and helpful. But my inquiry elicited a somewhat defensive and off-putting response from the program director:

> I have been doing adoptions from Poland for twenty-two years. Both of my children have come from the same orphanage as your daughter and neither of them have the problems that your daughter had.

She went on.

> I have sent your request to speak to us about our adoption program to our lead attorney in Warsaw. She will

discuss your request with the adoption authorities
and give us guidance on how to proceed. Please hold
off on contacting any more of our coordinators.

Several follow-up e-mails seeking clarification went unan-
swered.

Was I being told to back off? This wasn't a witch hunt. I was
a grieving father looking for answers.

My next contact was with an adoption group specializing
in Eastern Europe and Russia. Their initial response was more
muted but still tinged with suspicion.

While I understand your interest in gathering information, I cannot grant your request to speak to our
adoptive families at this time. We have to protect
the privacy of our membership. There are too many
scams in the world today, and they often come via
email. Information is simply too readily available
for me to accept your email as legitimate.

I called and left voice mails at several adoption groups in the
Bay Area but never heard from anyone. Perhaps they were busy
or, as I was beginning to discover, they might not have wanted
anything to do with me.

This was not the reception I was expecting.

As my search for answers to Casey's life and death continued,
I discovered a sad irony—every single person and institution in
the adoption chain means no harm, but their actions are often
harmful. They all want what they believe is best for the children.
However, ultimately, it seems that everyone who comes in contact with these children somehow fails them:

- Adoption agencies don't warn adoptive parents that institutionalized children may have severe behavioral problems, no matter how normal they seem or how quickly they catch up.
- Orphanage caregivers obey instructions to stay emotionally distant from the children.
- Adoptive parents, particularly those in foreign countries with limited fluency in the language and the legal system, don't ask questions for fear they will lose the child.
- Friends and family are too quick to tell concerned parents what they want to hear, that the tantrums and lack of affection are normal, a stage.
- Mental health experts, partly out of ignorance but sometimes out of professional arrogance, misdiagnose, lecture, fail to connect, ignore the elephant in the room (adoption), and may leave the child feeling even worse about herself, maybe even blaming her for not cooperating.
- Government agencies often erect impenetrable walls between the child and the birth parents, believing that respect for privacy is better for all concerned.

It doesn't have to be this way. Maybe it isn't everywhere. The adoption system is beginning to change. New therapies and parenting techniques are making their way into the mainstream. Dr. Marvin believes that these new ideas and practices can help mitigate the damage caused by separation and institutionalization, but they aren't a cure-all. "It's like being an alcoholic or suffering from a spinal cord injury or PTSD," he said. "The parents' job is to be the prosthetic to the child, to understand and accept that she'll have a different developmental path than most kids. She'll use that prosthetic to self-regulate."

Change to the adoption system needs to start earlier than postplacement, by which point the damage has already been done. Ray Kinney notes that prospective parents are becoming better informed about the spectrum of risks their child might face. He consults with more parents before they adopt a child, and provides specific instructions on how to handle the child in the early days, emphasizing that the child had a life before her adoptive parents received her. "It makes a world of difference when you can get to the parents before they even get on the plane," he said.

Vic wrote to me that Poland is transitioning from institutional orphanages to foster homes, where the children have a more predictable life and a closer connection with a dedicated caregiver. Open adoptions, where the birth parents have more control over their child's future, have become more accepted by prospective parents, but only for domestic adoptions.

He wrote about the process they went through with a young mother-to-be. He and Joanna discussed with her the pros and cons of keeping the baby versus adoption, and they decided together that adoption was preferable. They constructed a profile of the type of family the mother wanted for her child and searched an online Polish adoption forum for a couple who seemed to match the mother's profile.

Much like an open adoption in the United States, the mother and prospective parents met and got to know one another. They spent time together in the adoptive parents' home before and after the child's birth. The handover was done with minimal emotional trauma. The birth mother had a say in her child's future home, and the child had the knowledge that she was not abandoned, but rather carefully placed with a family that would be able to give her the kind of life her mother wished for her.

For sixteen years, I'd fantasized about meeting Casey's birth mother. Even though Casey claimed disinterest, I wanted to know what her mother looked like, observe her mannerisms, listen to the way she spoke, maybe meet Casey's siblings. In what ways were they like her?

I wanted to know who produced this child who had brought us so much joy, but who had also tested every ounce of our patience. I wanted to ask why she gave Casey up instead of another of her children. And who was Casey's birth father?

They could have taught us so many things about her daughter. Maybe knowing more would have made a difference.

# EPILOGUE

In the summer of 2008, just months after Casey's suicide, Erika and I joined an advocacy group fighting for a suicide barrier on the Golden Gate Bridge. We already knew that the bridge was a suicide destination for some people, but were stunned to hear that suicides from the Golden Gate dwarfed those from any other structure on Earth, more than 1,600 since it was built in 1937. Statistics have shown that suicides from the bridge ranged from thirty to forty-five annually since the mid-2000s. But those numbers double or triple if you count people who were rescued from the bridge. Despite these alarming statistics, public opinion in the Bay Area and that of many directors on the Bridge District Board had been decidedly against a suicide barrier for years.

In October 2008, after a long and contentious debate, the board voted fourteen to one in favor of installing a safety net on the bridge. But it was a hollow victory. There was no plan to fund the then-estimated $50 million project cost.

Nearly four years later, after intense lobbying from a coalition of families of bridge suicide victims, mental health professionals, and dedicated local politicians, Senators Barbara Boxer of California and James Inhofe of Oklahoma cosponsored a reauthorized, two-year Federal Transportation Bill that would provide a portion of the funding necessary for the suicide barrier. The bill was passed by the House and Senate in June 2012.

In June 2014, the Bridge District Board voted unanimously for a $76 million revised funding package from regional, state, and federal sources for the suicide barrier. Installation of the net is expected to commence sometime in 2016 with completion targeted for 2019. The persistence of the families of suicide victims remained key to moving this project forward.

Since Casey's suicide, more than two hundred people have leaped to their deaths from the Golden Gate Bridge. Every story is tragic, especially those of the younger victims.

For years, I blamed the bridge for Casey's death. If only there had been a barrier. But it was just an easily accessible means to act out on a destructive impulse. The larger question was what brought her there in the first place—not once but twice? I'll never know for certain—since Casey had never been properly evaluated or diagnosed—but the origins of her emotional problems can probably be traced to her infancy, and those problems were likely exacerbated by a steady stream of well-meaning but ill-informed people, from orphanage caregivers to therapists to us, her parents.

I've learned that the act of separating a mother from her baby is a traumatic experience for both. How could it not be? The process of adoption is far more complex and fraught with risk than we ever knew. In fact, some professionals dislike the tendency to overuse the terms *attachment disorder* and *reactive attachment disorder* as convenient labels for troubled adopted children. Because of the lack of reliable information at birth, many other issues can go undiagnosed—fetal alcohol syndrome, effects of drug addiction, and mental illnesses that could have been passed on by the biological parents.

While orphaned children, as a group, are at a higher risk for learning, emotional, and behavioral disorders than children raised by their birth family, not every adopted child suffers the effects of early deprivation. Many adapt to their new lives perfectly well and go on to live satisfying, productive lives in wonderfully loving adoptive families. Children can be amazingly resilient.

It wasn't until my own mother died from a massive stroke in October 2012 that I had a taste of being orphaned; my father had passed away in 2005. For a moment after hearing of my mother's death, I felt scared, lonely, and vulnerable. With my parents gone, who was going to take care of me? An irrational thought, of course, considering that I was a fifty-seven-year-old man. But imagine a terrified young child in the same circumstances. Even worse, what if her abandonment was not the result of death? Her parents were alive. They were out there somewhere, perhaps with other children of their own, while she was left behind. That was the reality into which my daughter was born.

Erika and I can't have a do-over. We can't have another Casey. But we hope that our story and lessons learned can help families and children, like ours, who are still alone and desperate for guidance.

# ACKNOWLEDGMENTS

This story began as a 450-page saga about a grieving father until I met Adair Lara, a former *San Francisco Chronicle* columnist, author of numerous books, and host of many memoir classes in the living room of her San Francisco Victorian home. She saw the story that I had completely missed—my search for answers to Casey's suicide—opening up an entirely different journey into attachment disorders in children who had suffered early-life trauma. I owe her a debt of gratitude for her vision and literary guidance.

I am deeply indebted to the team at Scribner, who took this story to an entirely different level. Adene Corns discovered me at a reading at our local Fairfax, California, library, and Roz Lippel and the Scribner editorial and production team in New York shaped and packaged this into an awesomely professional work for any reader's or bookseller's shelves. Scribner believed in this story when everyone else did not. It's exceptionally rare for a first-time author to make it into the publishing big leagues, but sometimes you get lucky.

# Acknowledgments

Many thanks to the adoption and attachment professionals who gave in to my repeated e-mails and voice mails and agreed to speak with me—Dr. Robert Marvin, Ray Kinney, Dr. Gregory Keck, Nancy Newton Verrier, Heather Forbes, Jane Brown, and Amy Klatzkin. Through a fortuitous online encounter, Vic Magnet of Agape Trust in Paslek, Poland, gave me an unusually comprehensive view of Polish orphan care.

I will be eternally grateful to Casey's friends, who've kept us going in the aftermath of her suicide. We've gathered together every year for fellowship, support, remembrance, and plain old fun, all of it in our own private ways. It's the one day Erika and I truly look forward to.

Finally, I thank Erika for sticking together as we try our best to navigate a different life without our Casey.

# RESOURCES

These are the resources and experts I came across in my journey. These listings are by no means meant to be a personal endorsement or all-inclusive. Rather, they can provide a starting point for readers to conduct their own exploration.

## BOOKS

Bowlby, John, *A Secure Base: Parent-Child Attachment and Healthy Human Development* (New York: Basic Books, 1988).

Brodzinsky, David M., *Being Adopted: The Lifelong Search for Self* (New York: Doubleday, 1992).

Gray, Deborah D., *Nurturing Adoptions: Creating Resilience after Neglect and Trauma* (Indianapolis, IN: Perspectives Press, 2007).

———, *Attaching in Adoption: Practical Tools for Today's Parents* (Indianapolis, IN: Perspectives Press, 2002).

Karen, Robert, *Becoming Attached: First Relationships and How They Shape Our Capacity to Love* (New York: Oxford University Press, 1998).

Keck, Gregory C., and Regina M. Kupecky, *Adopting the Hurt Child: Hope for Families with Special-Needs Kids* (Carol Stream, IL: NavPress, 1995).

# Resources

Keck, Gregory C., and Regina M. Kupecky, *Parenting the Hurt Child: Helping Adoptive Families Heal and Grow* (Carol Stream, IL: NavPress, 2002).

Magid, Ken, and Carole A. McKelvey, *High Risk: Children Without a Conscience* (New York: Bantam, 1988).

Meese, Ruth Lyn, *Children of Intercountry Adoptions in School: A Primer for Parents and Professionals* (Westport, CT: Bergin & Garvey, 2002).

Verrier, Nancy Newton, *The Primal Wound: Understanding the Adopted Child* (Lafayette, CA: Verrier Publications, 2003).

Verrier, Nancy Newton, *Coming Home to Self: The Adopted Child Grows Up* (Lafayette, CA: Verrier Publications, 2004).

## ONLINE MAGAZINES, SITES, AND BLOGS

ACEsConnection.com. A social network whose members use trauma-informed practices to prevent and lower adverse childhood experiences, and raise resilience.

ACEsTooHigh.com. A go-to site for news and information about adverse childhood experiences.

Adopting.com. An online resource for domestic and international adoption.

Adopting.org. Provides adoption articles, resources, and chat rooms.

Adoptionvoicesmagazine.com. A personal blog that includes posts, poetry, videos, and podcasts from a wide variety of voices from the adoption community.

Adoptivefamilies.com. The resource and community for adoption parenting.

Adoptivefamiliescircle.com. An online community touched by adoption to connect and share experiences.

Juliaandme.com. An adoptive mother's blog in which she shares about her adoption experience and adoption information in general.

Parentingandattachment.com. My own blog in which I share about my experience with Casey and lessons learned about adoption, parenting, and therapy techniques.

Chicagonow.com/portrait-of-an-adoption. A blog dedicated to sharing personal adoption stories.

Theadoptiveparent.com. A resource network for adoptive parents.

# Resources

## ARTICLES

Harlowe, Harry, "The Nature of Love," *American Psychologist* 13 (1958), 673–85: http://psychology.about.com/od/historyofpsychology/p/harlow_love.htm.

Rutter, Michael, "The English and Romanian Adoptee Study: Effects of Early Deprivation on Long-Term Adjustment" (1998), http://www.nuffieldfoundation.org/english-and-romanian-adoptee-study.

The Association for the Treatment and Training in the Attachment of Children, "Therapeutic Parenting" (2008), http://www.adoptiontoolbox.com/files/ATTACh_Therapeutic_Parenting_Handbook.pdf: m/b.

## ORGANIZATIONS

Adopt.org. The National Adoption Center, dedicated to expanding adoption opportunities for children living in foster care throughout the United States.

Agape-Trust.org. A charitable organization working with Polish orphans. Vic and Joanna Magnet, directors.

Americanadoptioncongress.org. The American Adoption Congress, an organization committed to adoption reform.

Theattachmentclinic.org. Mary D. Ainsworth Child-Parent Attachment Clinic at the University of Virginia Medical Center. Dr. Robert Marvin, director.

ATTACh.org. The Association for Treatment and Training in the Attachment of Children.

Attachment.org. Nancy Thomas Parenting, offering information on adoption, attachment, and bonding issues and early trauma to families and professionals.

Attachmentparenting.org. Attachment Parenting International is dedicated to educating and supporting parents, and offering resources for education and networking.

Attachmentparenting.co.uk. The U.K. resource for attachment parenting.

Attachmenttraumanetwork.com. The Attachment & Trauma Network, the nation's oldest parent-led organization supporting families of children with attachment disorders.

# Resources

Caseyfamilyservices.org. Established by the Annie E. Casey Foundation to provide pre- and postadoption services.

Childtrauma.org. The Child Trauma Academy provides information on the effects of child trauma and supportive interventions.

Psych.ucsf.edu/sfgh/ctrp. Child Trauma Research Center, UCSF/San Francisco General Hospital. Dr. Alicia Lieberman, director.

Adoptioninstitute.org. The Donaldson Adoption Institute, which provides adoption research and policy addressing the needs of those touched by adoption.

FRUA.org. Families For Russian and Ukrainian Adoption, offering family and adoption education resources, chatroom, social media connections, and a supportive community that nurtures adopted children and supports parents and families.

Rainbowkids.com. The Voice of Adoption, providing tools, resources, and guidance to those considering international adoption.

Nationalcenteronadoptionandpermanency.net. The National Center on Adoption and Permanency, dedicated to providing a broad range of services relating to adoption, foster care, and child welfare. Adam Pertman, president.

Theraplay.org. The Theraplay Institute, an international training institute.

## SPECIALISTS

Attachmentadoption.net. Family Attachment and Adoption Center, Oakland, CA. Virginia Keeler-Wolf, MA, MFT.

Beyondconsequences.com. Beyond Consequences Institute, Boulder, CO. Heather Forbes, director.

Comeunity.com/adoption/health/jenista.html. Jerri Ann Jenista, MD, Ann Arbor, MI.

Cornerstonecounseling.com. Cornerstone Counseling Services, Waukesha, WI. Ray Kinney, director.

Drfederici.com. Dr. Ronald Federici & Associates—Care For Children International, Manassas, VA.

Janebrowntoronto.weebly.com. Jane Brown's Adoption Playshops, Mississauga, Ontario. Jane Brown, MSW, director.